Confiteri
The Praise of a Soul

MW01016155

Shauna May

CONFITERI: THE PRAISE OF A SOUL
Copyright © 2015 by Shauna May

ISBN: 978-1-4866-1017-4   Printed in Canada

Word Alive Press
131 Cordite Road, Winnipeg, MB R3W 1S1
www.wordalivepress.ca

Cataloguing in Publication may be obtained through Library and Archives Canada

Gifted to

Thomas & Katrina

with love from

Davena

benediction

To God be the glory!

"God speaks to us in three places: in scripture, in our deepest selves, and in the voice of the stranger."
—Thomas Merton

Day 1

At one time we too were foolish, disobedient,
deceived and enslaved by all kinds of passions and
pleasures ... He saved us through the washing of
rebirth and renewal by the Holy Spirit.
—Titus 3:3, NIV

Lord, understanding both the problems of human nature and Your response to it, I see that I have a choice: either I can accept or reject Your wisdom. Acceptance promises renewal. And, if everyone experienced renewal, society would be transformed! How can I not choose You?

Day 2

To the lady chosen by God and to
her children, whom I love in the truth
… I ask that we love one another. And this
is love: that we walk in obedience
to his commands.
—2 JOHN 1:1, 6

*Ah, how often I favour one over the other. Some days I am all truth;
other days, all love. Won't You shake me up, Lord? Give these vital
elements a good stir. Blend them together so that, for once, I pour them
out in proper proportion!*

≈

Day 3

He protected us on our entire journey …
—JOSHUA 24:17

*You tell us to be prepared and ready for great things to come. We learn
to brave new frontiers with courage, to swim against the tides, to fight
our battles with promise. You are victorious, and You will take us as
far and as deep as we are willing to go. May I fall deeply into You.*

Day 4

Do not stare at me because I am dark,
because I am darkened by the sun.
—SONG OF SONGS 1:6

O God, uphold me; establish my heart in thy faith! How I have gazed upon You, loved You, prayed to You, and here I am again, writing to You with a passion inspired by torturous inquietudes. No one is as beautiful, as understanding, as loyal as You. How I would do anything for Your sake!

Day 5

This is the Good News about Jesus
the Messiah, the Son of God.
—MARK 1:1

The Servant comes to serve, to suffer, to save—everyone but Himself. And in one act, the continued life of humanity is made possible. As I lay my burdens down at your feet today, my tortured soul feels as if it has wings. I will never fully know why my brightest day had to be Your darkest one. True, it is from a place of sober, heart-wrenching gratitude that I thank You today.

Shauna May

Day 6

CONTEMPLATIVE PRAYER
… we can't help but thank God for you, because your faith is flourishing and your love for one another is growing. We proudly tell God's other churches about your endurance and faithfulness in all the persecutions and hardships you are suffering.
—2 THESSALONIANS 1:3, 4

Lord, help me to fan the flames of faith in others. May their faith grow exceedingly strong, and our love continually increase. How precious the burning ember of faith, may it ne'er be extinguished!

Day 7

I long to see you again, for I remember your tears as we parted. And I will be filled with joy when we are together again.
—2 TIMOTHY 1:4

Lord, I can only pray that my children, fleshly and spiritual, will always know the tears and the joys they have brought me. May they know how deeply proud I am of them, every single day. Lo, I shall tell them as much today!

4

Day 8

No foreigners, including those who
live among the people of Israel, will
enter my sanctuary if they have
not ... surrendered themselves
to the Lord.
—EZEKIEL 44:9

Lord, let my heart hold nothing back. Let me surrender my all that I may experience all of Thee!

⸺

Day 9

There is none righteous, no, not one ...
—ROMANS 3:10, NKJV

I am forgiven and I can live righteously by faith in Christ. The beautiful thing is, You give me the power to do it. And I have learned that the more I rely upon You, the greater I can increase this power. I can live according to will and not feelings. I can be better, do better. Is that not the most promising hope in the world?

Day 10

In the beginning God ...
—GENESIS 1:1

As the divine Author, You show us where and how it all began, sketching scenes of short-lived paradisiac harmony with promise of life eternal. Despair, competition, strife, inadequacy takes root as soon as mankind parts ways with You, their Creator. Still, You provide hints of a beautiful ending in store. How gracious You are!

Day 11

... put on the new self, created
after the likeness of God in true
righteousness and holiness.
—EPHESIANS 4:24, ESV

The human self was created, fallen, redeemed, and is now capable of being made new! My mind, my character, my relationships can be made new, made after your likeness still. How wonderful is that? How marvelous are You!

Day 12

... that their hearts may be encouraged, being knit
together in love, to reach all the riches of full
assurance of understanding and the knowledge
of God's mystery, which is Christ ...
—COLOSSIANS 2:2, ESV

Lord, let no distance separate the smile in our hearts or loosen the bonds of love that connect us in faith. May we grow together in our triumphs and spoils as we strive earnestly to emulate You. For have You not purposed that we should be brought closer together in Your likeness?

Day 13

But solid food belongs to those who are of full age,
that is, those who by reason of use have their senses
exercised to discern both good and evil.
—HEBREWS 5:14, NKJV

Lord, by meditating and reasoning upon Your Word, I build solid roots—roots that keep my spirituality from withering under heat. However, there are times I prefer to reach my own conclusions. Forgive me when that is the case, and guide my attempts to better discern Your will.

Day 14

People judge by outward appearance,
but the Lord looks at the heart.
—1 SAMUEL 16:7

*Appearances don't matter to You, Lord. Names, titles, bank accounts,
shells: immaterial assets we cling to, yet matter not at all in the great
scheme of things. All You see is our spirit within. You alone see the
heart. What a relief! What a comfort. What a blessed thing is that?*

Day 15

God ... chose to bring many children into glory.
And it was only right that he should make Jesus,
through his suffering, a perfect leader, fit to
bring them into their salvation.
—HEBREWS 2:10

*Lord, thank you for countless revelations: for Your Word, for Your
Word made manifest in Christ, for making LOVE known by the sufferings of Christ. When I fix my eyes on You, I feel as though I am
peering into the eyes of love itself, and for that gift, I praise Thee!*

Day 16

Let the word of Christ dwell in you richly, teaching
and admonishing one another in all wisdom,
singing psalms and hymns and spiritual songs,
with thankfulness in your hearts to God.
—COLOSSIANS 3:16, ESV

*O, the depths of Your wisdom and knowledge! How You peel back
the layers of my frightened soul and flood my heart with Your beauteous presence. Now pour out of me in song Lord, that all will hear
and know Your magnificence and splendor. Let us love You for Your
own name sake!*

Day 17

... what sort of people ought you to be in lives of
holiness and godliness ...
—2 PETER 3:11, ESV

*"Have you ever considered the force of a habit in your life?
Nothing is more powerful than the patterning or
programming of your life and thoughts by habit.
It draws you to the same seat when you enter church."*
—HAROLD SALA

Day 18

Let your heart therefore be wholly true …
—1 Kings 8:61, ESV

My true self is what was created, what Christ came to redeem and affirm. My false self is that which Christ came to destroy. Therefore, let me be fearless in affirming my calling as Your created one. And let my heart be wholly true!

≈

Day 19

Rejoice and be exceedingly glad, for great
is your reward in heaven, for so they
persecuted the prophets who
were before you.
—Matthew 5:12, NKJV

When all around me gives way, my joy cannot. Lord, let it shine so bright it looks like the glory of Heaven's descent to earth. This joy, THIS, is what the world longs for without even knowing it. It is this joy that makes great our reward to come!

Day 20

We know that we are children of God
and that the world around us is
under the control of the evil one.
—1 JOHN 5:19

Protect me, Father, from the lures of the world around. Everywhere I turn I see a lure, and with each lure is a hook; with each hook is the falsehood that I must satisfy fleshly needs over spiritual. O, please help me avoid such enticements today!

Day 21

For this light momentary affliction is preparing for us
an eternal weight of glory beyond all comparison ...
—2 CORINTHIANS 4:17, ESV

In hard times, Lord, I am reminded of the work You began in me. I wish not for trials and afflictions, and if I could, I would beg You to remove them, except that I know You use them to strengthen and develop your servants. O Lord, let me endure!

Day 22

Then the Lord God said, "It is not good for
the man to be alone. I will make a helper
who is just right for him."
—GENESIS 2:18

God, help me serve as a complement, in word and deed; to be an honorable witness to the work You are doing in, around, and through me. And to You be the glory and honour, forever and ever, amen.

≈

Day 23

When it was clear that we couldn't
persuade him, we gave up and said,
"The Lord's will be done."
—ACTS 21:14

Let me not be easily swayed to the left or to the right, Lord. But with eyes on You, let me shake off the dust of discouragement and bravely press on. Even in my deepest groaning, let not mine, but Your, will be done.

Day 24

... and sometimes you helped others who
were suffering the same things.
—HEBREWS 10:33

Father, I have found tremendous power in communicating with You. Prayer lets me better relate to myself, and the better I relate to myself, the better I can relate to others. In fact, the more open I am with You, the more expansive my love is for others. In essence, the more I heal, the more I help. How kind of You to bless me through prayer!

Day 25

He shouted at the top of his voice, "What do you
want with me, Jesus, Son of the Most High God?
In God's name don't torture me!"
—MARK 5:7, NIV

O, God of eternal comfort and strength, is this tortured man not an amalgam of all the pain and suffering of society today? Is he not a mirror of ourselves? Is he not shouting out the very pain we carry? Please, Lord, hear my weeping. Answer my prayer!

Day 26

We serve God whether people honor us
or despise us, whether they slander us
or praise us. We are honest, but
they call us impostors.
—2 CORINTHIANS 6:8

Woe to me if I had no enemies! Woe if all spoke well of me! You see those who ridicule me. You hear their taunts. You bear my shame. You unshackle chains of degradation and loosen the ties that scorn and despise. Thank God, Lord, that I have You by my side!

Day 27

For by a single offering he has perfected for all
time those who are being sanctified.
—HEBREWS 10:14, ESV

By giving us Your Son, in that one selfless act of love, guilt was pushed aside for all men. If guilt is pushed out of my heart, should that not make more room for love? Why then do I still wrestle with it intense feeling of guilt, Lord?

Day 28

... teaching them to observe all that I
have commanded you.
—MATTHEW 28:20, ESV

Father, when I hear all around me Your words of truth and those words alone, and when I can imagine no other, then will I know I am beginning to observe You. Lord, for me to be able to think and be irresistibly carried away by Your thoughts alone, to be unable to think or speak anything but what You have put in my mind and mouth—that would be a striking feat!

Day 29

For this my son was dead, and is alive
again; he was lost, and is found.
—LUKE 15:24

If I am partly the result of creation and partly the result of fallen, defaced mankind, then if I deny my fallen self—all that is incompatible with You—and affirm my created self—all that is compatible with You—will I more closely resemble the person I was destined to be? Must I lose my fallen self to find my created self? If this is so, let the old self fall away at once!

Day 30

This is my body, which is given for you.
—1 CORINTHIANS 11:24

And he took a cup of wine and gave thanks
to God for it. He gave it to them, and
they all drank from it.
—MARK 14:23

You bore my sins. I am sorry You had to. It shames me, and I pray I never trample on Your sacrifice. Without it, I'd give out from the weight of my burdens. Instead, I draw strength from it. How can I ever repay You?

Day 31

I appeal to you therefore, brothers, by the
mercies of God, to present your bodies as
a living sacrifice, holy and acceptable to
God, which is your spiritual worship.
—ROMANS 12:1, ESV

Father, You lovingly take my timid hand in Yours. You cradle this broken heart. You see my cracks and crevices and promise to make them whole. You accept me as I am. And so now Lord, I pray that I may accept Your acceptance of me, and thus make peace with myself.

Day 32

If God is for us, who can be against us?
—ROMANS 8:31, ESV

Have You not given me wreath upon wreath of victory? Do You not lift my face upward, time and time again? Is there a battle made impossible without You? No, for when your sword is strapped to my thigh I feel at once mighty of heart! You are my all and all. Thank you, Lord, thank you.

Day 33

… as you share in our sufferings, you will also
share in the comfort God gives us.
—2 Corinthians 1:7

You desire for us to share suffering, don't You, Lord? You would not have us be self-enclosed or distanced from society, yet this is my immediate response to suffering. Knowing Your desire, why do I still make suffering a secret? Why do I rob myself of the comfort You wish to give? When will I learn?

Day 34

When Jesus got out of the boat, a man with an
impure spirit came from the tombs to meet
him. This man lived in the tombs, and no
one could bind him anymore, not
even with a chain.
—Mark 5:2–3, NIV

This story breaks me, Lord. Such a social outcast was this man—he was living in the tombs? And people had tried to bind him, even with chains? Can you imagine the misery and sadness? How did he endure? Where is peace then?

Day 35

But when you ask him, be sure that your faith is
in God alone. Do not waver, for a person with
divided loyalty is as unsettled as a wave of the
sea that is blown and tossed by the wind.
—JAMES 1:6

*Lord, You taught me how to pursue. You pursued me fiercely! And
now it is I who chases after You. Loyally I cling to You, for without
You my life would have no meaning. You are all this heart yearns to
think upon!*

Day 36

When he saw the crowds, he had compassion on
them because they were confused and helpless,
like sheep without a shepherd.
—MATTHEW 9:36

*O, God, I regret being so swayed by my own needs, worries, and ten-
sions that I fail to attend to the needs of others. Lord, when I am constantly elsewhere in my thoughts and intentions, how can I possibly be
of help to those in need? Allow me to withdraw from my own activ-
ities, my world of stimuli—real or perceived—and intensely concen-
trate on others. In Your name I pray.*

Day 37

To him who loves us and has freed us
from our sins by his blood ...
—REVELATION 1:5, NIV

You love me well, yet I give you no reason. I can barely contain the liberation and healing that comes from that kind of love. Indeed, I pray only for the courage to love and forgive others as freely as You do. You have my hand and heart, Lord, now let me open them wide to others.

≈

Day 38

You are fairer than the sons of men;
Grace is poured upon Your lips;
Therefore God has blessed
You forever.
—PSALM 45:2, NASB

Indeed, Lord, You are the fairest of all; most graceful, too. Your obedience unto death, your unwavering faithfulness, makes You beautiful. Raised and blessed with immortal life seals Your beauty for all eternity. Eagerly, I await a glimpse ...

Day 39

LORD, look down from heaven; look from your holy,
glorious home, and see us. Where is the passion and
the might you used to show on our behalf?
—Isaiah 63:15

*"Find the courage to enter into the core of Your own existence and
become familiar with the complexities of Your own inner lives ...
discover the dark corners as well as the light spots, the closed
doors will evaporate, our anxiety will diminish and we
will become capable of creative work."*
—Henri Nouwen (*Wounded Healer*, 42)

Day 40

The Lord bless you and keep you ... be gracious
to you ... and give you peace.
—Numbers 6:24–26, NIV

*Lord, prepare my heart for an encounter with You today. Let me feel
Your smile beam inside of me, radiating outward, setting free the songs
that have held my soul captive O so long. Awaken my spirit. Set my
heart aglow. Let it rain everlasting kindness today!*

Day 41

Spread out your home, and spare no expense!
For you will soon be bursting at the seams.
—ISAIAH 54:2–3

Lord, I have named my disgraces, called out my fears, wallowed in shame, and lamented my sorrows. Invade me, Lord. Occupy my soul to the point I am bursting at the seams. And I promise to fear not your entry.

≈

Day 42

But after a while the brook dried up, for there
was no rainfall anywhere in the land.
—1 KINGS 17:7

If I have not been drinking from the living fountain of your Word, the inner streams of my faith will falter. Forgive me, Lord. Bring me back to You. Unfold the petals of my soul with Your Spirit. Let me dwell in You that I may breathe again.

Day 43

So Jesus said to the Jews who had believed him, "If
you abide in my word, you are truly my disciples."
—JOHN 8:31, ESV

*Lord, where can I go that You will not find me? When my conscience
plagues and I hide from your Light, when I bury myself deep into
darkness, do you not always lift me out? Why? Why, then, do I flee
when the joy is always greater at Your side?*

≈

Day 44

Now concerning spiritual gifts ... no one
can say "Jesus is Lord" except in the Holy
Spirit. Now there are varieties of gifts, but
the same Spirit; and there are varieties
of service, but the same Lord.
—1 CORINTHIANS 12:1, 3–4, ESV

*Lord, how thankful I am that You pour your Spirit out generously
upon all who ask of it. Desperately I ask that the Spirit You poured in
me may now work for Your good.*

Day 45

... following the stubborn desires of their evil hearts.
They went backward instead of forward.
—JEREMIAH 7:24

Merciful Father, everywhere I go I see blurred images of sexuality, skewed senses of morality and irrationality, lack of impulse control, fascination with darkness, disregard for creation, antisocial tendencies, undeveloped potentials, and a grave amount of worship not of You. O, Father, will me to move forward. Let me not be trapped in the old, but be made new in You!

≈

Day 46

The family heads ... and everyone whose heart
God had moved—prepared to go up and build
the house of the Lord in Jerusalem.
—EZRA 1:5, NIV

O, God, how You restore and stir my heart! When I stray, You hear my deep-seated cries for return, and rebuild my crumbling defenses. Thank you for divorcing me from anger and grudges, lust and coveting, that I may find in You that which I love and which satisfies above all else.

Day 47

... but he tore the chains apart and broke the irons
on his feet. No one was strong enough to
subdue him. Night and day among the
tombs and in the hills he would cry
out and cut himself with stones.
—MARK 5:4–5, NIV

How heart-breaking is this? How often was this man chained? What strength inspired by pain! I can almost hear him howling out in torment, desperate to express his pain and suffering. So great his misery, he was a threat unto himself! Why must relief be elusive for so long?

Day 48

There was an immediate bond between them,
for Jonathan loved David.
—1 SAMUEL 18:1

I think You have revealed to me through Your Word, Father, that love for self and love for others are intricately tied together—embryonically so. You designed us for bonds of fellowship. May I strengthen the ties that bind. Inspire us to come together for Your name's sake. Thank you, Lord!

Day 49

And let us consider how to stir up one
another to love and good works ...
—HEBREWS 10:24, ESV

*Lord, please stir up a pot of human kindness and pour it into the
mouths of Your people through me today. Let them feel as I do when
You open my heart and pour loving kindness into me. Let them burst
forth with joy and be moved to praise You, my God of Gods, my Pro-
vider, my Life-Joy!*

≈

Day 50

... all of you are children of the Most High.
—PSALM 82:6, KJV

*Heavenly Father, remind this child of Yours who she is today: where
she has come from, from whom she has heard the truth, and to know
where in life she is going! Help me to remember remembrances that I
may later call them to mind with renewed joy and fondness. In Your
name, I pray.*

Day 51

So you are no longer a slave, but a son, and if
a son, then an heir through God.
—GALATIANS 4:7, ESV

... and if children, then heirs—heirs of God
and fellow heirs with Christ.
—ROMANS 8:17, ESV

*Who am I, but an heir of God, a fellow heir of Christ, an heir to the
throne! Indeed, being a created, fallen, redeemed human is a trans-
forming experience—one that transforms into glory. Hallelujah, and
again I shout, hallelujah!*

Day 52

What will be the sign that the Lord will heal me ...?
—2 KINGS 20:8, NIV

*To be ostracized, considered a threat even unto myself, pales com-
pared to the shame of knowing I've done things to break the relationships I hold most dear; to live with the guilt of hurting the very ones
I loved most, how do I? Lord, tell me, from whence and wither does
healing come?*

Day 53

And suddenly there came from heaven a
sound like a mighty rushing wind, and
it filled the entire house where they
were sitting ... And they were all
filled with the Holy Spirit ...
—Acts 2:1, 4, ESV

Dear children, let's not merely say that
we love each other; let us show
the truth by our actions.
—1 John 3:18

When You call me "dear child," I smile. Thank you, Father. Now, may I remember to talk less and act more today! May I not be known as a "walking sermon," but rather let me reach hearts and souls through selfless action. Lord, may this spirit flourish to Your praise and to Your glory. Amen!

Day 54

O Lord, you have examined my heart
and know everything about me.
—Psalms 139:1

Lord, I'm sorry. Be with me.

Day 55

Now I rejoice in my sufferings for your sake …
—COLOSSIANS 1:24, ESV

Lord, if I am to suffer, can I not help others despite my suffering? Though I suffer, I have enormous love for people, and desire them to be happy. Can I not use this love to help them suffer less? You have taught me that the significance of my life corresponds exactly to my suffering: this, THIS, is cause for rejoicing!

≈

Day 56

Be of good courage, and let us be strong
for our people and for the cities of our
God. And may the Lord do what
is good in His sight.
—2 SAMUEL 10:12, NKJV

Grant me courage, Father, to do what is good in Your sight, not what I perceive to be good or right! You have a right to do as You please with what You own. Do with me what is needed for Your coming glory.

Day 57

... let your good deeds shine out for all to
see, so that everyone will praise
your heavenly Father.
—MATTHEW 5:16

*Your wisdom is the light of our souls. I have caught just a glimpse,
my Father, and it is so, so glorious that it has left my heart a flutter.
Please, let my passion shine bright enough to ignite the path of others
on this journey.*

Day 58

We patiently endure troubles and hardships and
calamities of every kind. We have been beaten,
been put in prison, faced angry mobs, worked
to exhaustion, endured sleepless nights,
and gone without food.
—2 CORINTHIANS 6:4–5

*O, how they think bubbliness and buoyancy comes without a care! Do
they not know, Lord, that exuberance comes out of every single affliction and out of every sleepless night I have felt You near? Would they
hear these sighs? Would they believe You have wiped my every tear?*

Day 59

And I myself will be a wall of fire around it
... and I will be its glory within.
—ZECHARIAH 2:5, NIV

As olive tree branches drip oil into lampstands to burn ever-brightly, so too, You infuse my inner being with the light of Your Spirit that my faith, amid a world of darkness, shall burn ever-brightly. Thank you, my God of Gods, for I am all the stronger for it.

≈

Day 60

For the secret power of lawlessness
is already at work ...
—2 THESSALONIANS 2:7, NIV

To the degree I vanquish impropriety in my own heart will determine the degree to which You will use me to vanquish it in the world around. This is no time to be idle. This is the time for planting, sowing, watering and ... warning. The joy of reaping shall come tomorrow!

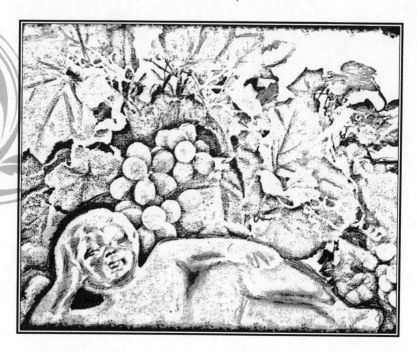

Day 61

May the God of endurance and encouragement
grant you to live in such harmony with one
another, in accord with Christ Jesus ...
—ROMANS 15:5, ESV

I dreamt today of a world residing in harmony, at peace with one other, with all of creation, with ourselves, and with You. How much longer, Lord, must I dream? My heart laments sorrows seen. When will You rain down peace? How much longer are we to endure?

Day 62

PRAYER PARTNERS
For we don't live for ourselves
or die for ourselves.
—ROMANS 14:7

God, please forgive me for the many times I choose things over people. Forgive me for showing signs of annoyance when interrupted, and for failing to prioritize the gift of life. May I better appreciate memory-making moments in the dew of all the little things that refresh the heart, and let not this heart be heavy. Thanks be unto Thee!

≈

Day 63

He must hold firm to the trustworthy word
as taught, so that he may be able to give
instruction in sound doctrine and also
to rebuke those who contradict it.
—TITUS 1:9, ESV

Let me ne'er depart from Your Word! How greatly I delight in it. Teach me to handle it aright, always submitting to the Spirit in humility and trust. You are truth my God, and I shall honour You in my prayer, in my wanderings, in my studies. I shall honour You always!

Day 64

Only do not rebel against the Lord, nor fear
the people of the land, for they are our bread;
their protection has departed from
them, and the Lord is with us.
—NUMBERS 14:9, NKJV

Father, free this quivering heart from fearing man and seeking his approval. O, how it weakens my strength! Truly, there is no substitute for Your approval, Your blessing, Your protection. Happy am I when I seek You alone.

Day 65

And I was with you in weakness and in fear
and much trembling ... that your faith
might not rest in the wisdom of men
but in the power of God.
—1 CORINTHIANS 2:3, 5, ESV

You are always with me, Lord. In every season, I am made strong by the power of Your irresistible light. You are the God of all consolation, and how comforted I am that You are "with us always, even to the end of the age." Lord, carry me in your arms today!

Day 66

Faith—more precious than gold that
perishes ... is tested by fire.
—1 PETER 1:7, NKJV

*The more our faith is tried by fire, the more valuable we become. The
more we are tested, the more our endurance grows; the more we burn,
the more dazzling our virtues shine thereafter; and the more brightly
we shine, the more clearly the world sees You!*

≈

Day 67

But for your sake we are killed every day;
we are being slaughtered like sheep.
—PSALM 44:22

*A life of faith is not without ridicule. If they berated your Son, they
will berate me also. Yet I would be blind not to see a noble purpose in
this. Thus, I pray that I may honour "the crucified life" in all I do. And
I thank You. Truly, this is an esteemed privilege I do not take lightly.*

And you, who were dead …God made alive
together with him, having forgiven us all
our trespasses, by canceling the record
of debt …This he set aside,
nailing it to the cross.
—COLOSSIANS 2:13–14, ESV

You took my guilt and all the effects of it—the self-pity, depression, failed relationships, addictions, and placed them in the palm of your Son's hand, which was nailed to the cross. And You did all this for me? O, the power of Your love, Your unfailing grace—how can it be?

Day 69

Anxiety in a man's heart weighs him down,
but a good word makes him glad.
—PROVERBS 12:25, ESV

O, how a good word comforts and raises a dejected soul! How it charms one's frets into sweet and quiet thoughts, frees it from the anxieties of this world, and keeps it fixed upon things that are above. Do let my endearments be nothing but sacred today, dear Lord. For this, I thank thee!

Day 70

Shall tribulation, or distress, or persecution, or
famine, or nakedness, or danger, or sword?
—ROMANS 8:35, ESV

*Only one thing can separate me from Your love and that is myself. I
perish the thought that my pride or insecurities should ever thwart
something so very precious. Allow me the grace, my Father, to make
mistakes but to always, always return to You. In Your name I pray.*

≈

Day 71

He's a glutton and a drunkard, and a friend
of tax collectors and other sinners!
—MATTHEW 11:19

*Where would we find You today? In palaces or marching in parades,
in churches and chapels or in grungy skateboard parks, bowling al-
leys, playgrounds and parks? Would You mingle with the poor in spirit, or hobnob with lords and leaders? Would I delight in the Son of
Man in You?*

Day 72

Therefore encourage one another and build
one another up, just as you are doing.
—1 Thessalonians 5:11, ESV

May I encourage with constancy, for it can a mere second to tear down what I have built up, and the precious hearts of your people are too dear to destroy. These are gorgeous lives in the making—lives seeking You—lives made more beautiful in You, of You, and for You. O, how I thank You for each one!

Day 73

For you have been called to live in
freedom, my brothers and sisters.
—Galatians 5:13

I wasn't free when You called me, Father. I was bound to another cause. And while it was not hard to choose You over and against, it was a leap of faith that scared me to death. I felt certain to fall; certain to fail. But You ensured I fared well. O, God of my heart, art Thou not faithful as promised?

Day 74

Look at the birds ... aren't you far
more valuable to him than they are?
—MATTHEW 6:26

And how much more valuable
is a person than a sheep!
—MATTHEW 12:12

It is sometimes hard to believe that You would regard us as more valuable than beasts and the crown of your creation, yet if made in Your image, we must be of distinctive value. Thank you for seeing me that way, O God of Creation. Thank you for declaring me "good!"

Day 75

Finally, brothers, whatever is true, whatever is
honorable, whatever is just, whatever is pure,
whatever is lovely, whatever is commendable, if
there is any excellence, if there is anything
worthy of praise, think about these things.
—PHILIPPIANS 4:8, ESV

Let me simply think upon You, for is it not Your thoughts, Your ways, that fill me with inexpressible joy and infuse my raging mind with peace? Blessed be You that You are God!

Day 76

... in all these things we are
more than conquerors ...
—ROMANS 8:32, ESV

IN all these things, I have more than conquered. IN afflictions, IN suffering, IN sorrow, IN risks taken, IN faith lived out, IN loyalty to You, I have more than conquered because I have life in You now and am assured of a greater one to come. With that, I softly pray, "All is well with my soul."

≈

Day 77

Let the whole earth sing to the Lord!
Sing to the Lord; praise his name.
—PSALM 96:1–2

Lord, should I ever engage in listless worship, forgive me! You deserve better—You deserve the best. Help release disquieting thoughts when I come before You in praise. Let the bosom place of my soul be filled with nothing but blissful, rhythmic silence offered to You in a beauteous new song. Thank you. Thank you for all the amazing things You do. Lord, how I love You!

Day 78

... sorrowful, yet always rejoicing ...
—2 CORINTHIANS 6:10, NIV

O, it is easy to talk about joy in sorrow, yet impossible to experience without the Holy Spirit. Thus I pray, Lord, when my mind is troubled, that You shall replenish my cup with the wine of the Spirit and reassure me that "Christ hath shed his own blood for my soul," and that, indeed, all is well.

Day 79

You have made heaven, the heaven of
heavens, with all their host, the earth
and all that is on it, the seas and all
that is in them; and you preserve
all of them; and the host of
heaven worships you.
—NEHEMIAH 9:6, ESV

Not only did You create everything with astonishing beauty, but You gave Earth the amazing ability to sustain itself. It is no small wonder that the heavenly hosts praise You. Lord, may I too!

Day 80

We know that we are children of God,
and that the world around us is under
the control of the evil one.
—1 JOHN 5:19

Protect me, Father, from the lures of the world around. Everywhere I turn I see a lure, and with each lure is a hook; with each hook is the falsehood that I must satisfy fleshly needs over spiritual. O, please help me avoid such enticements today!

≈

Day 81

... but my brothers who went with me frightened the
people from entering the Promised Land.
For my part, I wholeheartedly followed
the LORD my God.
—JOSHUA 14:8

Always you ask, "Will you follow Me when you are frightened as well as when you are brave? Will you follow Me when you are healthy as well as when you feel poorly? Will you follow Me in light as well as in darkness?" God, I hope so!

Day 82

LITURGICAL PRAYER
... your kingdom come, let your will be done,
on earth as it is heaven.
—MATTHEW 6:10, NIV

Let Your will be done on earth, on Earth, as it is in Heaven, Father. May Your gorgeous green footstool release a sweet odour as an offering to You. May Your healing touch of love and compassion reach and inspire us to feel more deeply, to respond with respect, and to seek divine means by which we the people of this small but precious Earth become one to one another.

≈

Day 83

And Jesus replied, "I assure you, today
you will be with me in paradise."
—LUKE 23:43

How I wish I was in paradise today! Lord, without that promise where would I be? So I say, thank you for giving me this paradisiac hope—hope that points to an end of suffering, mourning, and pain. It points to a life with You. And for that reason, I can face today.

Day 84

The glory of this present house will be
greater than the glory of the former house
... and in this place I will grant peace.
—HAGGAI 2:9, NIV

Inhabit me, Lord. Make Your dwelling-place in my heart that I shall one day know what it feels like in Heaven! Be my master. Be my guide. Beautify the sanctuary of my soul.

Day 85

You make the clouds your chariot;
you ride upon the wings of the wind.
—PSALM 104:3

If we cannot create a spirit of belonging among ourselves in close-knit community, how can we do that with all of creation? As one of your worldwide "children of Light," may I be infused with a heartfelt desire to serve the needs of this wounded earth more fully. Allow my inner being to be touched once more by your Spirit—the very Spirit of Life that "rides upon the wings of the wind!"

Day 86

And the Spirit and the bride say, "Come!" And
let him who hears say, "Come!" And let
him who thirsts come. Whoever desires,
let him take the water of life freely.
—REVELATION 22:17, NKJV

"Come, take life's water free!" Almighty God, I can't speculate how much longer this invitation is extended, so without haste, let me respond! Hear my gratitude in the praise I offer You! O, restorer of paradise lost, let the heavens rejoice! Let the earth grateful be! Come, Lord Jesus. Let many more "take life's water free."

Day 87

God keeps such people so busy enjoying life that
they take no time to brood over the past.
—ECCLESIASTES 5:20

It's funny how the idea of wanting to eradicate past suffering can become such a preoccupation that it becomes more and more fixated. I wonder, Lord, if I were to become more preoccupied with You and with acts of goodness, would I be so joyously engaged I'd have no time to brood?

Day 88

Fear the Lord your God, and live in a way
that pleases him, and love him and serve
him with all your heart and soul.
—DEUTERONOMY 10:12

*Father, may You give through my hands, smile through my eyes, and
open my heart to bless those You desire to be blessed. It is when I give
of my entire heart and soul that I truly please You. With heartfelt
praise I thank You and exalt You, great giver of life.*

Day 89

Bear one another's burdens, and
so fulfill the law of Christ.
—GALATIANS 6:2, ESV

*I don't know how I fulfill the law of Christ by bearing another's bur-
dens, but if You say that is so, then Lord, let me carry ten times my
weight! Bring people to me. Let me comfort and support them. Let me
carry their load as You do mine . . . every single day. And thank you
for doing so!*

Day 90

BREATH PRAYER
See, God has come to save me. I will trust in him
and not be afraid. The Lord God is my strength
and my song; he has given me victory.
—ISAIAH 12:2

Leaning in, do I hear the soft sound of wind words? Yes, in an ever so still, ever so quiet voice, they are saying, "I am your salvation. Trust Me. Fear not one thing, for I am your strength and your might!"

Day 91

... clothe yourselves with humility toward one
another, because, "God opposes the proud
but shows favor to the humble."
—1 PETER 5:5, NIV

Lord, You showed humility more than You spoke about it. You are the suffering servant. Indeed, washing the feet of Your disciples left such an indelible mark that thirty years later Peter writes about it. Thus, I pray I may be humble in dealing with others not just today, but every day, Father.

B·U·D·D·Y
(BŮD'T) N. A. GOOD
FRIEND. A COMPATRIOT.
OR A PARTNER.

Day 92

I looked, and I saw a windstorm coming out of the
north—an immense cloud with flashing lightning
and surrounded by brilliant light.
—EZEKIEL 1:4, NIV

*O, to be Ezekiel, to witness your irresistible power and splendour! Is
it no wonder his heart was set ablaze? Lord, on an intimate scale, do
unto me as You have done in the history of this world. May your river
of life flow through me that I may know now what awaits me in the
life to come.*

Day 93

... she continued praying.
—1 Samuel 1:12, ESV

Years I have prayed without signs of change. Mountains still tower. Valleys run deep. Shadows haunt. Am I still to pray on?

Yes, my dear. Whether far or near, you must pray for signs of hope made clear!

Day 94

Do not keep talking so proudly or let your
mouth speak such arrogance, for the
LORD is a God who knows, and by
him deeds are weighed.
—1 Samuel 2:3, NIV

Who do You see in this heart of mine, Jahweh: Saul or David? Am I led by faith or by flesh, by carnal or by spiritual desires? Woe am I if the flesh wins out! Such a waste of opportunity! Let not this life be a tragedy, Lord. Please, increase my spirit of faith!

Day 95

Be fruitful and multiply. Fill the
earth and govern it.
—GENESIS 1:28

Lord, how great Thou art! How wondrous Thy creative works, and how humbled and honoured I am to care for the earth. Heighten my sense of responsibility. Help me to better care! Instill in all of us, Lord, the desire to serve and to protect creation.

≈

Day 96

Please pardon the iniquity of this people, according
to the greatness of your steadfast love.
—NUMBERS 14:19, ESV

Lord, before the cross I see our worth: the greatness of Christ's love in His sacrificial death. At the same time I am confronted with our unworthiness: that we caused Your Son to die. Forgive us, Father. Ignite our desire to receive of Your good grace. And let us now love. Amen.

Day 97

FASTING PRAYER
Just as we are now like the earthly man, we will
someday be like the heavenly man.
—1 CORINTHIANS 15:49

*Lord and Father, help me see time spent with You as an opportunity
to let go, to be, rejoice in NOT doing. Truly, it is impossible for me to
duplicate what You did on my behalf. But, because you did, and because you live, I have hope that one day I shall be fully me, no longer
emptied out or burdened.*

Day 98

Therefore, having been justified by faith, we have
peace with God through our Lord Jesus Christ...
—ROMANS 5:1, NASB

There is therefore now no condemnation for
those who are in Christ Jesus.
—ROMANS 8:1, ESV

*Ah, by faith in Christ, I have peace. By faith in Christ, I am set free. By
faith in Christ, I am forgiven. You wouldn't fool me, Lord. Is it truly
as simply as receiving Him? If so, I shall receive Him every day, every
hour, every minute of my life! Let Him be my Saviour forever!*

Shauna May

Day 99

He broke the power of death and illuminated
the way to life and immortality
through the Good News.
—2 TIMOTHY 1:10

Truly, You urge me to be a valiant torch-bearer! The gift of faith in our Saviour, Christ Jesus, must not die out. Help me keep the embers of truth alive in myself and in one another. Lord, what a privilege it is to blaze the path that Paul ignited centuries ago! May I delight in this always.

≈

Day 100

You know how I carried you on eagles' wings
and brought you to myself. Now if you
will obey me ... you will be my
own special treasure.
—EXODUS 19:4–5

Lord, You direct my spiritual pilgrimage daily. You never cease carrying me on "eagle's wings." Will me to grow in faith and to obey You and to always feel your loving arms wrapped round me. Thank you, my God of Gods, for daily protection!

Day 101

Looking at the man, Jesus felt genuine love for him.
—MARK 10:21

… Jesus loved Martha, Mary, and Lazarus …
—JOHN 11:5

Let the children come to me … For the Kingdom of
God belongs to those who are like these children.
—LUKE 18:16

The attitude which Your Son displayed to men, women, and children reveals how greatly we, as humans, matter. By simply loving us, You raised our value. How often do I seek to find my worth, yet You keep seeking to make me worthy. Most blessed am I!

Day 102

PRAYERS OF RECOLLECTION
Come to Me, all who are weary and heavy-laden,
and I will give you rest.
—MATTHEW 11:28, NASB

Rest sounds so good, so very good. Why do we busy ourselves in doing, when truly all that is asked of us is to come and soak up love at the feet of our Master? God, pour Yourself into me that I may refresh others just as abundantly.

Day 103

Prepare to meet your God …
—Amos 4:12

Why me, Lord?

"My sweet child, why not you? If bad things befall some, why shouldn't they befall you as well?"

So, if I expect troublesome things, I shouldn't be so surprised when they occur, right, Father? Is this your way of preparing me to face life with more confidence?

"Yes, my child. Now, prepare to meet your God."

≈

Day 104

The word of the LORD to Israel through Malachi,
"I have loved you," says the LORD.
—Malachi 1:1-2, NIV

Malachi, to your freed people of Babylon, has the final voice for four hundred years. What does he say? Look to the future: see Jesus Christ, Sun of Righteousness, who "will rise with healing in its wings." Unsurprisingly, you wrap the Old Testament up with the message, "I have loved you." Let us echo that.

Day 105

Wherever you go, I will go; wherever you live,
I will live. Your people will be my people,
and your God will be my God.
—RUTH 1:16

As I ponder Ruth's loyalty in her moment of crisis, I am overwhelmed with respect. She chose not to be defeated by grief. She chose togetherness over solitude. She chose You over false gods. And look how You blessed her! Is it any wonder she is named as an ancestress of Jesus?

Day 106

For what is your life? It is even a vapor that appears
for a little time and then vanishes away. Instead
you ought to say, "If the Lord wills, we
shall live and do this or that."
—JAMES 4:14–15, NKJV

My life is not in me. It is in Christ. Indeed, if I lose this earthly life, I shall have gained another. Let it be Your will then, God of my heart, how I shall live and what I shall become.

Day 107

O Lord, you know; remember me and visit me,
and take vengeance for me on my persecutors. In
your forbearance take me not away; know that for
your sake I bear reproach. Your words were found,
and I ate them, and your words became to me a
joy and the delight of my heart, for I am called
by your name, O Lord, God of hosts.
—JEREMIAH 15:15–16, ESV

*Lord, You are my Balm of Gilead, the soothing salve for my sin-sick
soul; infuse me with the raw honesty, heroic courage, and iron determination of Jeremiah, for I delight to bear Your name!*

Day 108

[I] will rejoice over you with gladness... quiet you
with [my] love ... rejoice over you with singing.
—ZEPHANIAH 3:17, NKJV

*How is Zephaniah able to paint You with brushstrokes of black and
white, but I am ridiculed when I see the world that way, Lord?*
    *"Ah, because my love is greater than yours. Though I judge your
sin, I see your pain, and purify you. After your punishment, don't you
see? My justice is superior, but so is my love.*

Day 109

For God knew his people in advance, and he
chose them to become like his Son, so that his
Son would be the firstborn among
many brothers and sisters.
—ROMANS 8:29

Lord, I want to be spiritually transformed. I want to train wisely toward that end. I want to complement the brother and sisterhood of Christ. I want to complement You! Help me never swerve off the path that leads to You, for this is life. This is the real life—the happy, purposeful life. This is the life of Christ, and I thank you for showing me the way.

Day 110

Repent for the kingdom of heaven is at hand.
—Matthew 4:17, ESV

Where there is a king, there is a kingdom. Behold our King! He mounts a donkey, wields a broken reed, and is crowned with thorns; gathers a following; asks that we surrender to Him in every aspect of our lives; is enthroned in our hearts and, in a limited sense, we experience kingdom come. And what a wonderful phenomenon is that?

Day 111

Now go; I will help you speak and
will teach you what to say.
—Exodus 4:12, NIV

Ah, the story picks up speed! You reveal a baby born under a sentence of death—Moses, who miraculously survives and goes on to lead a small remnant into promised relationship with You. In Moses, You show us that all we need to accomplish things in Your name is You— just You. With You as our confidence, how then can we not sing of Your praise?

≈

Day 112

You are to be holy [whole] to me because I, the
LORD, am holy [whole], and I have set you
apart from the nations to be my own.
—Leviticus 20:26, NIV

You are Holy; You make me whole. Early into this story, You tell us exactly how we are to approach You, your Holiness. You invite us to do so. In trust, some willing believers respond. You sanctify them, set them apart as a people for your name. Will You likewise, in your holiness, make me Yours, make me whole?

Day 113

The LORD gave and the LORD has taken away;
may the name of the LORD be praised.
—JOB 1:21, NIV

But he knows the way that I take; when he has
tested me, I will come forth as gold.
—JOB 23:10, NIV

Why, Lord? Why do we insist on finding a spiritual reason for suffering? Can we not accept your training, feel privileged, and not bitter? Father, even as I suffer, hear my triumphant song, "I will come forth as gold!"

Day 114

But we know that when Christ appears, we shall
be like him, for we shall see him as he is. All who have
this hope in him purify themselves, just as he is pure.
—1 JOHN 3:2–3, NIV

I will only purify what I think needs purifying! Let me see the mirror of another's perceptions before me, that I not remain blind to my failings. Lord, let me confess my faults—my pride and jealousy—and humble myself before You. To Godlikeness I aspire, for 'tis You who inspires!

Day 115

If a man has a hundred sheep and one of them
wanders away, what will he do? Won't he leave
the ninety-nine others on the hills and go out
to search for the one that is lost?
—MATTHEW 18:12

The great shepherd, Christ Jesus, who would brave hardship and risk peril to seek and to save one lost sheep, must surely consider all humans to be of extreme value! You sent Him to serve, to suffer, to die for us—for me. How insolent of me to not see my worth!

≈

Day 116

For I wrote you out of great distress and anguish of
heart and with many tears, not to grieve you but to
let you know the depth of my love for you.
—2 CORINTHIANS 2:4, NIV

I love the depth of emotion Paul pours into the 2 Corinthians. O, that ministers today would feel as free to show their vulnerabilities, their anxiety, and agitations! Is it not in our weakness that we are strong? Indeed, Lord, let them see me weak, that they will then see You!

Day 117

We always thank God for all of you and
continually mention you in our
prayers ... your endurance inspired
by hope in our Lord Jesus Christ.
—1 Thessalonians 1:2–3

*Thank you, Jahweh. Today, I take heart and have hope. Your Son is
returning. The flowers are blooming. You're in the heavens, and all is
right with the world.*

Day 118

Holy, holy, holy is the LORD Almighty;
the whole earth is full of his glory.
—Isaiah 6:3, NIV

*How could a human being like me write a book as exalting of Your
majesty and power as Isaiah? What did he see and know of Your immensity, infinite might, and holiness that I have not? Why, You were everything to Isaiah, my Eternal Father. Won't You be everything to me?*

Day 119

... tell them how much the Lord has done for
you, and how he has had mercy on you.
—MARK 5:19, NIV

*Lord, I marvel at Jesus' touch. He commands relief, and it is felt im-
mediately! Be it physical, emotional, social, or in the healing of memories, You touch us in ways that healing occurs. O, God of Peace, what
will come of my unceasing prayers? Shall I see You in my healing, too?*

Day 120

How long, O LORD, must I call for
help? But you do not listen!
—HABAKKUK 1:2

*Lord, I cry out to You and hear no answer! "I hear you. Perhaps My
answer is just not the one you were seeking. Have you not wondered if
the problem is the answer? Step back. Wait. Look again. Now what
do you see?" I see myself carrying on, regardless. "Good. 'Though it
linger, wait for it; it will certainly come and will not delay.'"*

Day 121

Don't be afraid ... for God has come in this way
to test you, and so that your fear of him
will keep you from sinning!
—EXODUS 20:20

Help me, Father, to be more like Moses: meek yet courageous. Though filled with fear, he stepped out boldly for Your name's sake. Is that not the truest form of courage? O, Lord, may I not be afraid to be tested, but respond with boldness, come what may.

≈

Day 122

The God whom we serve is able to save us ...
But even if he doesn't, we want to make it clear
to you, Your Majesty, that we will never
serve your gods or worship the gold
statue you have set up.
—DANIEL 3:17–18

Am I willing to risk ALL for You? Am I that loyal, that trusting, that firm in faith I'd relinquish this very life for Your cause? You are my life. Why would I hesitate?

Day 123

So never be ashamed to tell others about our Lord.
And don't be ashamed of me, either, even though
I'm in prison for him. With the strength God
gives you, be ready to suffer with me for
the sake of the Good News.
—2 TIMOTHY 1:8

*O, Lord, my personal frailties may give cause for shame, but may the
Good News never! Let me reflect today on the legacy that I shall leave
behind. O, how I pray it is example-worthy!*

Day 124

The wall was completed ... in fifty-two days. When
all our enemies heard about this all the surrounding
nations were afraid ... they realized that this work
had been done with the help of our God.
—NEHEMIAH 6:15–16, NIV

*Lord, let me stop and remember how You have reconstructed my
walls, how You reinstruct my mind, and how You renew this heart
daily. You still the sounds and reverberations of these lingering memories. Never are You too distant from my soul. Alive and active, You are.*

Day 125

INTERCESSORY PRAYER
But the Holy Spirit prays for us with groanings
that cannot be expressed in words.
—ROMANS 8:26

*Lord, in interceding for others, our winged soul takes flight, lifting it
up and outward, and away from self—ever pleading, ever beseeching.
And for the work of the Holy Spirit, who groans on our behalf when
mortal words utterly fail us, Lord, thank you and praise You! Amen.*

Day 126

In truth I perceive that God shows no partiality.
—ACTS 10:34, NKJV

*Tell me, with complete candor my Father, do I have a reputation
for being impartial? Do traces of racial, social, or economic partiality linger in my heart? Lord, I earnestly pray for You to reveal my
feelings. I beg You to adjust my attitude that I may reflect Your im-
partiality to a fuller degree. Let me see people, all people, as You see
them. Thank you, Lord.*

Day 127

"Please don't leave us," Moses pleaded. "You
know the places in the wilderness where we
should camp. Come, be our guide."
—NUMBERS 10:31

*You draw your people out of bondage, protect them in their wilderness
wanderings, refine them in the deserts of discipline, and guide them
toward a haven of peace and rest. Your unwearyingly patience moves
me, inspires me to yield completely, and stills the nervous palpitations
of my heart.*

≈

Day 128

I have great sorrow and unceasing anguish in my
heart. For I could wish that I myself were cursed
and cut off from Christ for the sake of my
people, those of my own race ...
—ROMANS 9: 2, NIV

*Lord, you have enlivened my heart and soothed my spirit. Now let me
weep with those who weep. Add to the grace in my tears, deep love.
And let nothing stand in the way of joyful living!*

Day 129

Surely God is good ... to those
who are pure in heart.
—PSALM 73:1, NIV

O, how weak a thing the heart of a human. Too fragile, too forgetful, too fearful, yet still You see purity in it. How can it be? That realization bursts my heart, Lord. How incomparable is Thy goodness!

≈

Day 130

Fear not, for I am with you ... I will strengthen
you, I will help you, I will uphold you
with my righteous right hand.
—ISAIAH 41:10, ESV

If I have faith in Your promises, great God of deliverance, ought I not to fear less? With less fear, should this heart of mine not abound more in love? If that is so, then Lord, strip away my fears so that love is all that remains within me!

"for now we see through a glass darkly..."

Day 131

And the child grew and became strong; he was filled
with wisdom, and the grace of God was on him.
—LUKE 2:40, NIV

*O Light of my heart, it is You I am starved for, for in You is truth. In
You is beauty and wisdom. In You, is divine favour. I stand humbly
before You, Lord, for in You this soul of mine seeks to live!*

Day 132

May the God of hope fill you with all joy and peace
in believing, so that by the power of the Holy
Spirit you may abound in hope.
—ROMANS 15:13, ESV

*You touch me and I have peace. You smile upon me and I have joy.
You see my faith and I am forgiven. Your Spirit breaks my chains and
frees my soul. And I am beholden unto You, Ancient of Days, for still
You make new!*

Day 133

... you answer our prayers. All of
us must come to you.
—PSALM 65:2

*Lord, let not a spirit of ingratitude dominate me, but let me praise
You with thanksgiving, day in and day out! For the times I murmur
or complain, forgive me. And Lord, please let grateful prayers rule this
household that my children only learn thankfulness, and thus, resist
the spirit of this world. Thank You, Father.*

Day 134

... you have searched me and known me.
—Psalm 139:1, ESV

Lord, examine my heart! Show me how to peer deeply into my soul, reflect on my lifestyle and unburden belongings. Give me strength to strip away the mental and physical debris that clutter my streams of spiritual consciousness. May things not anchor me, but rather propel me in kingdom pursuit!

Day 135

Then we who are alive, who are left, will be
caught up together with them in the clouds
to meet the Lord in the air, and so we
will always be with the Lord.
—1 Thessalonians 4:17, ESV

I live to be caught up by You, Lord, to flee from perils of the flesh; to have my inner temple cleansed; to have my angst quelled. O, to behold this world no more! Come down, Lord. Come down!

Day 136

But the Lord is with me as a mighty, awesome One.
—JEREMIAH 20:11, NKJV

Lord, Your evaluation of me is what counts, not that of men. There isn't a single accomplishment I can boast in, for all I have done has been by Your might. Men place value on our accomplishments, but You, Lord, You look at our faithfulness—and for that, I am so very, very grateful! I pray that I may remain faithful.

≈

Day 137

For from within, out of a person's heart,
come evil thoughts, sexual immorality, theft,
murder, adultery, greed, wickedness, deceit,
lustful desires, envy, slander, pride, and
foolishness. All these vile things come
from within; they are what defile you.
—MARK 7:21–23

With such ugly things in the human heart, will I ever reach my full potential in this life? O, what I wouldn't do to cast off everything in order to become light enough to follow You!

Day 138

... for the Son of Man has come to seek and
to save that which was lost.
—Luke 19:10, NKJV

As the time approached for him to be taken up to
heaven, Jesus resolutely set out for Jerusalem.
—Luke 9:51, NIV

*The Son of Man came to seek and to save what was lost—not "the
lost," but what was lost: the essence of mankind, the created image of
perfection ... the mystery we keep searching for and can never find,
never remediate. He found it. He fixed it. What more can I say? By
You, I exist!*

Day 139

... except that the Holy Spirit testifies in every city,
saying that chains and tribulations await me.
—Acts 20:23, NKJV

*Praise triumphs over tribulation. Music lifts the soul that we may see
higher peaks from a distance. When chains threaten to bind, from
within or without, it is then we must sing. It is then we must break the
depths of silence!*

Day 140

For the word of God is alive and powerful. It is
sharper than the sharpest two-edged sword, cutting
between soul and spirit, between joint and marrow.
It exposes our innermost thoughts and desires.
—HEBREWS 4:12

*What else has power to move or change or stir the hearts and souls of
men, but You? I open my Bible and find principles of love, faith, and
hope: principles that have made martyrs out of men—principles for
living a rich and meaningful life. Lord, thank you, for Your Word is,
indeed, life.*

Day 141

YOU ARE MY TEACHER
Oh, that their hearts would be inclined to fear me and
keep all my commands always, so that it might go
well with them and their children forever!
—DEUTERONOMY 5:29, NIV

*O, how forgetful we mortals are! Were we to simply listen and obey,
life would have been so much easier. With infinite tenderness You
pull us back to You, time after time. Let us remember You, Your
deeds, Your patience, Your love, that our hopes may blossom and our
dreams be fulfilled.*

Day 142

The Son of Man … feasts and drinks, and
you say, "He's a glutton and a drunkard,
and a friend of tax collectors
and other sinners!"
—MATTHEW 11:19

*If You came today, would I recognize You? Would I see in You what
the lowly saw? Would I embrace you, or reject One so radically different as You?*

≈

Day 143

I will praise the Lord no matter what
happens. I will constantly speak
of his glories and grace.
—PSALM 34:1, TLB

*Your Word speaks to us all differently. It meets us exactly where we are
at, several times a day. That is the beauty of it; that makes Your Word
come to life! Through it You fuel our passion for life, for You, for one
another. To You be the glory and honour forever, amen.*

Day 144

How much more will those who receive God's
abundant provision of grace and of the gift of
righteousness reign in life through the
one man, Jesus Christ!
—ROMANS 5:17, NIV

*Do I see myself deeply-seated in Christ's heavenly realms? Do I not
know that You have filled my sin-drenched self in every way? Surely,
if I fail it is because I have not appropriated what is already mine.
God, let me not be stingy, but take all that these hands and heart can
grasp of you!*

Day 145

My brothers and sisters, if one of you should wander
from the truth and someone should bring that person
back, remember this: Whoever turns a sinner from
the error of their way will save them from death
and cover over a multitude of sins.
—JAMES 5:19–20, NIV

*To sit someone down and explain their error with the intent of win-
ning them over is love in action. O, how I have been hurt by the opposite approach. Lord, let me strive to speak truth in love today!*

Day 146

To the faithful you show yourself faithful; to those
with integrity you show integrity. To the pure
you show yourself pure, but to the crooked
you show yourself shrewd.
—2 SAMUEL 22:26–27

So many, the mirrors. No matter how hard or how long I try, I still fall so readily. Why, Lord? Indeed, why did King David? How do I forgo formalities and live more authentically? Become to me what I am to You!

≈

Day 147

He has besieged me and surrounded me
with bitterness and hardship.
—LAMENTATIONS 3:5, NIV

Yes, I have been grieved by suffering, heartache, and desolation of spirit, but there is always a purpose in what You do. You use even our pain and sorrow. What are You emboldening, empowering me for? Should I not praise You, ever-faithful One, that I am a part of your plan?

Day 148

For all creation is waiting eagerly for that
future day when God will reveal
who his children really are.
—ROMANS 8:19

Father, forgive us, for we have sinned. We suffer when creation suffers, and yet it is our sin that causes creation to suffer! This we know. For my part, I confess the error of my ways, and pray that earthly healing begins. Lord, open my eyes, unstop my ears, refine my heart, and please point the way forward so that ALL creation may praise You indefinitely!"

≈

Day 149

I am writing you these instructions so that, if I am
delayed, you will know how people ought to
conduct themselves in God's household,
which is the church of the living God,
the pillar and foundation of the truth.
—1 TIMOTHY 3:14–15, NIV

O, that streams of unceasing love would flow from a Church of pure hearts bathed in good conscience standing before You, the living God of our faith. May Your grace be with us!

Day 150

Why all this weeping? You are breaking my heart!
I am ready not only to be jailed at Jerusalem but
even to die for the sake of the Lord Jesus.
—ACTS 21:13

*Should I die in kingdom service I will have risen that much closer to
You, will have become more like You, will have accomplished my life's
goal. Still, I cling to this foolish life. Lord, command me to let go and
live a full throttled life for You!*

≈

Day 151

Beloved, we are God's children now ...
—1 JOHN 3:2, ESV

By this all people will know that you are my disciples ...
—JOHN 13:35, ESV

Or do you not know that your body is a temple of the
Holy Spirit within you, whom you have from God?
—1 CORINTHIANS 6:19, ESV

*Who am I, but a child of Yours, a disciple, a home of the Holy Spirit.
You have opened my soul to self-discovery, and by this, granted me a
glimpse of my worth. How can I ever thank Thee?*

Day 152

There is only one thing worth being concerned
about. Mary has discovered it, and it will
not be taken away from her.
—LUKE 10:42

Troubled. Well-intentioned. Hospitable. Loving. Skilled. Over-
whelmed. Tired. Unnoticed. Dear Lord, Martha is me, except she
knew to ask for help. I ask You for help all the time, Lord. Why can't
I ask that of people? Why must I be so proud? Can I not simply sit at
Your feet and be?

≈

Day 153

But none of these things move me; nor do I count
my life dear to myself, so that I may finish my race
with joy, and the ministry which I received from
the Lord Jesus, to testify to the gospel
of the grace of God.
—ACTS 20:24, NKJV

Heaven forbid that I chase after earthly treasures. Lord, I beg You
to steer my feet resolutely toward You, for nothing in this world can
compare to the endless joy that is found in You.

Day 154

Two are better than one, because they have a good
reward for their toil … though a man might
prevail against one who is alone, two will
withstand him—a threefold cord
is not quickly broken.
—ECCLESIASTES 4:9–12, ESV

*You will always be my better half, Lord. With You as the third cord in
any union, it shan't be broken. You are stronger than me. Your love is
greater. You fortify all my relationships, and for this, I exalt You!*

Day 155

Therefore, if anyone is in Christ, he is a
new creation. The old has passed away;
behold, the new has come.
—2 CORINTHIANS 5:17, ESV

*Lord, the body aches. The soul tires. The mind grieves. It is hard to feel
like a new creation at times. I wonder if You would especially let me
feel it today! Thank You, Father. In You I trust.*

Day 156

We are honest, but they call us
impostors. We are ignored, even
though we are well known.
—2 CORINTHIANS 6:8–9

They may call me names, be indifferent, ignore my actions, but they cannot kill my joy. For in my heart of hearts, I know You care. You want me to win. And though I am surrounded by loneliness, I rejoice, for I have never felt closer to You! Blessed be Thy name.

≈

Day 157

CENTREING PRAYER
The one thing I ask ... is to live in the
house of the Lord all the days of my life,
delighting in the Lord's perfections
and meditating in his Temple.
—PSALM 27:4

Lord, possess me as Yours. My only hope is to remain in Your quieting presence that the I may hear Your voice, feel it, sense it, know it, live it, be changed by it—changed by Your mercy.

Day 158

I lift up my eyes to the hills. From where does
my help come? My help comes from the Lord …
he who keeps you will not slumber. The Lord
is your keeper; the Lord is your
shade on your right hand.
—Psalm 121:1–5, ESV

I look and all I see is You, my soul's tireless keeper, the One who slumbers not, so that in my brightest day or my most dreadful night, I am guarded by the protective span of Your out-stretched wings, and O, how I desire to soar underneath them!

Day 159

If you love me, obey my commandments.
—John 14:15

Lord, I am afraid if I cling too tightly to rituals they will become gods unto themselves—negating any good I attempt to do. How easy it is to do all the right things for all the wrong reasons, Lord. Should that happen my life will seem not harmonious, but joyless. O, Lord, keep me honest, please!

Day 160

And Judas and Silas, who were themselves
prophets, encouraged and strengthened
the brothers with many words.
—ACTS 15:32, ESV

*Countless are the times words have restored to me thoughts of joy in
times of weakness. Today, Lord of my heart, will You let me repay that
gift? May I be cognizant of delivering words that raise the affections of
another's heart, and quicken their graces of zeal and gratitude.*

≈

Day 161

... learn to do good; seek justice, correct
oppression; bring justice to the fatherless,
plead the widow's cause.
—ISAIAH 1:17, ESV

*Make use of my voice! Use it to speak in behalf of those who cannot,
those whose will has been broken, those whose case needs pleading. O,
Lord, use me to show this world that You see their pain, that You hear
their cries, that You feel their plight, and that an end is in sight!*

Day 162

If any of you wants to be my follower, you must
turn from your selfish ways, take up
your cross, and follow me.
—Matthew 16:24

*Lord, Your spirit of self-sacrifice knows no limit. Is selflessness not the
heart of worship? The love you showed, Jesus, drives every other virtue; it demands selflessness. It is the defining mark of a true disciple.
May it define me!*

Day 163

Come, let us return to the Lord. He has torn us to
pieces but he will heal us; he has injured us but he will
bind up our wounds ... As surely as the sun rises, he
will appear; he will come to us like the winter rains,
like the spring rains that water the earth.
—Hosea 6:1, 3, NIV

*Your story, Lord, is one of love—a love that erases shame, renews zeal,
and blooms human beauty into hope and restoration without end.*

Day 164

For if you remain silent at this time, relief and
deliverance for the Jews will arise from another place,
but you and your father's family will perish. And who
knows but that you have come to your royal
position for such a time as this?
—ESTHER 4:14, NIV

*How do I rule over the warring kingdom of my soul, the will that sits
proudly 'pon its throne, and a spirit which longs for You? O, Lord, give
me courage to hand over my secret wars to love!*

Day 165

... do this in remembrance of Me.
—1 CORINTHIANS 11:24, NIV

It is just after sundown. The clouds lift and I see the crescent of the moon. You are about to die that I may be crowned with Your loving kindness and tender mercies. Your body breaks that I may be made whole. I beseech you, Lord, for words that would express how I feel. Perhaps a word of silence most fits this day.

≈

Day 166

What wrong did your fathers find
in me that they went far from me,
and went after worthlessness,
and became worthless?
—JEREMIAH 2:5, ESV

I most feel my worth when I give of myself. When I hold a child, paint flowers with her, weave braids through her hair, sing and dance with her, show her how to love You, then I know my worth, for it is directly tied to You!

Day 167

The message of the cross is foolish to those who are
headed for destruction! But we who are being
saved know it is the very power of God.
—1 CORINTHIANS 1:18

*Ah, all that I tend to think matters—praise, acceptance from the
world—matters not! Impressing others is wisdom to the world, but
foolishness to You! Only when I learn to appreciate the difference in
source, flesh over spirit, can I grasp the knowledge and wisdom that
empowers, saves, makes whole. Amen for that!*

Day 168

For what is our hope or joy or crown of boasting
before our Lord Jesus at his coming? Is it not you?
—1 THESSALONIANS 2:19, ESV

*By changing me, You change my fallen, disparaging self-image. You
have given me more to affirm. Permit me to do so not braggingly, but
gratefully. And now, Lord, two wonders I confess: the glory of the
Cross, and my own unworthiness!*

Day 169

Then He said to them all, "If anyone desires to
come after Me, let him deny himself, and take
up his cross daily, and follow Me."
—LUKE 9:23, NKJV

*If I renounce my fallen self—this corruptible, finite, mortal self—will
I the more plenteously discover my created self—the self that was
made in Your glorious image? Will I learn to appreciate human nature as You do? Divine One, illumine me, please, that I may know and
love like Thee!*

Day 170

And do not get drunk with wine ... but be filled with
the Spirit, addressing one another in psalms and
hymns and spiritual songs, singing and making
melody to the Lord with your heart ...
—EPHESIANS 5:18, ESV

*My soul thirsts for You, Lord. I beg You to fill my cup with the wine of
Your love and mercy till it overfloweth, for I cannot drink too much of
Thee. The more I taste, the more I crave. And as You fill me, hear this
heart make sweet melody to Your name!*

Day 171

They were stoned, they were sawn in two, they
were killed with the sword. They went about in skins
of sheep and goats, destitute, afflicted, mistreated—of
whom the world was not worthy—wandering
about in deserts and mountains, and in
dens and caves of the earth.
—HEBREWS 11:37–38, ESV

*The world is not worthy of those mistreated for the cause of Christ.
But we have worth in Your eyes. Is that not a reason to smile every
hour of the day, and every day of the month?*

Day 172

So let's humble ourselves ... and
surrender to the king of Israel.
—1 KINGS 20:31

*Let me submit my will, my desires, my emotions to Your will, Your
desires, Your kingdom that I may best fulfill my inward potential. Let
me see what You see in me, be who You destined me to be. Come, Lord,
reign in my heart!*

Day 173

CONTEMPLATIVE PRAYER
... Do not sorrow, for the joy of
the Lord is your strength.
—NEHEMIAH 8:10, NKJV

I am grateful to live by a sanctity that is inexpressibly intimate, to know that the gift of life is a portion of the breath and spirit of You, dear God. To dwell with You is to sense holiness of life, and to experience joy of life in Your presence—joy that comes when I remove distractions and allow myself to know that in You all things are true.

Day 174

Our hearts ache, but we always have joy.
—2 CORINTHIANS 6:10

Lord, I wish the world could see less pain, less painless joy, and more rejoicing in sorrow. I wish that those who taste heartbreak, ill-health, and loss, may not just ache, but ache with joy as they also taste Your goodness daily. Clothe my pain with joy that the world will turn to You!

Day 175

Those who are wise will shine like the brightness
of the heavens, and those who lead many to
righteousness, like the stars forever and ever.
—DANIEL 12:3, NIV

*Lions can't consume me; fiery furnaces cannot scorch; and there is not
a king alive that could separate me from Your love. It would take more
than that to pluck my soul out from the midst of Your presence. Now,
if I can only get through the troubles and calamities of everyday life . . .*

≈

Day 176

This is my body, which is given for you.
—1 CORINTHIANS 11:24

And he took a cup of wine and gave thanks
to God for it. He gave it to them, and
they all drank from it.
—MARK 14:23

*You bore my sins. I am sorry You had to. It shames me, and I pray
I never trample on Your sacrifice. Without it, I'd give out from the
weight of my burdens. Instead, I draw strength from it. How can I
ever repay You?*

Day 177

Let no corrupting talk come out of your mouths,
but only such as is good for building up
…that it may give grace to those who hear.
—EPHESIANS 4:29, ESV

This mouth begs to impart grace. I ask that You put Your words in my mouth. Let my utterances be sweet as honey, soothing like the healing balm of Gilead—life-giving to those who listen! Lord, I thank you for kindly words. I cherish them as I cherish YOU.

≈

Day 178

Protect me, for I am devoted to you. Save me, for I
serve you and trust you. You are my God.
—PSALM 86:2

Once I came to know You, trust You, serve You, feel Your mighty saving power, how could I not choose You? O beautiful God, there in none like You! How proud this heart is that it had enough sense to see and feel and act. Never have I been so proud!

Day 179

... but the Spirit gives life.
—2 Corinthians 3:6, NIV

How blessedly does art emerge from spiritual crises! Lord, you bestow me wellbeing in poor health—physical and emotional—but especially so when I lead a true life of the Spirit. To be more spirit than flesh is a strange fate; at times, a crushing fate, and I beg Your patience in living it well.

≈

Day 180

A word fitly spoken is like apples of
gold in a setting of silver.
—Proverbs 25:11, ESV

I pray Your Spirit puts upon my tongue words that will turn the mist of this world into sun, words this lonely world longs to hear: "You are not alone. Your needs are seen and felt. You are precious to me. Draw near to me and I shall draw near to you." Fill me, dear Lord with such words of hope!

Day 181

Put on your sword, O mighty warrior!
You are so glorious, so majestic!
—PSALM 45:3

You proved victorious over death, and so might we. With Your Word as a sword, we take our stand, valiant and strong. We will rise. We will overcome. We shall reign with You on High. Your today becomes our eternity. And in praise of Your splendour and majesty, my heart cries out, a blessed Hallelujah!

Day 182

"Put away your sword," Jesus told him. "Those
who use the sword will die by the sword."
—MATTHEW 26:52

In preferring the power of the sword to the power of love, have we rejected the way of the cross, Lord? Have we sought war over peace? And what of I? Have I chosen love over hate today? Lord, I know the answer to that, and hence, confess, repent, and pray. May I willingly commit to the way of love, always!

Day 183

You are the most handsome of all. Gracious
words stream from your lips. God himself
has blessed you forever.
—PSALM 45:2

God, You hear me. You see me. You love me. I know Your voice and
delight in hearing Your blessing. You have filled me with grace, and I
shall laud You forever. And dearest reader, I bless you.

Day 184

The blessing of the LORD makes a person
rich, and he adds no sorrow with it.
—PROVERBS 10:22

Trust takes work, Father. But I know if I meditate on Your works—
past, present and future—my trust in You shall be unbreakable; and
the more I trust, the more I shall praise and honour You. That is
what makes one rich, spiritually rich, my Father, and THAT is a
blessing galore!

Day 185

But recall the former days when, after you
were enlightened, you endured a hard
struggle with sufferings...
—HEBREWS 10:32, ESV

You never said that life would be a rose garden. And I have never ceased wondering why some suffer more than others, or why it is that spiritual anguish causes suffering so. But I do know that You have forgiven me and that You bless my spiritual activity, and that alone is reason for indescribable happiness.

≈

Day 186

We are poor, but we give spiritual riches to others.
We own nothing, and yet we have everything.
—2 CORINTHIANS 6:10

I own nothing but have everything if I have joy in suffering. Though lowly in the eyes of society, I am made rich in truth. You feed the gnawing hunger in my heart, and quench my thirst for eternal sayings. Indeed, I am rich among men!

Day 187

For God has not given us a spirit of fear and timidity,
but of power, love, and self-discipline.
—2 Timothy 1:7

Is it no small wonder I am encouraged to "fan into flame" these faithful qualities? As I do so, Lord, may it be not with a "spirit of fear and timidity," but with a powerfully bold and loving spirit—thus, alighting lives and hearts of men and women from here to eternity!"

≈

Day 188

Hear my prayer, O Lord, and give ear to my cry.
—Psalm 39:12, ESV

O, Hearer of Prayer, I come before your great and mighty throne with earnestness. Mostly I write and talk about subjects I feel qualified to address—not so now. This week I want to approach the matter of inner peace, particularly as applies to obtaining it. Show me the verses that will help me, please.

Day 189

INNER HEALING PRAYER

Now may the God of peace make you
holy in every way …
—1 THESSALONIANS 5:23

Lord, thank you for being with me, remaining with me and touching me with Your love. Help me to rely more fully on You, Lord, to walk with my feet firmly planted on the terra vita and with eyes on the beatific heavenly vision, for when the earth makes final claim to my limbs, 'tis then I shall truly dance!

Day 190

We love because he first loved us. If anyone says, "I
love God," yet hates his brother, he is a liar …
Whoever loves God must also love his brother.
—1 JOHN 4:19–21, ESV

Lord, the world cares not for what I don't do. It only cares for what I do. And at the end of the day, all that counts is how well, and how far, and how deeply, I have loved. Just as You lavish me with love, will me to love the least lovable, I pray!

Day 191

We prove ourselves by our purity, our understanding,
our patience, our kindness, by the Holy Spirit
within us, and by our sincere love.
—2 Corinthians 6:6

If I am patient and kind and loving in spirit, they marvel that I have not been broken. Yet what am I, but a bundle of joy wrapped up in sorrow? Is it not Your Spirit that works to produce patience over self-pity and kindness over revenge? Indeed, it is not I they see, but You in me!

≈

Day 192

Let my cry come before You, O Lord …
Let Your hand be ready to help me;
Let my soul live and praise you;
—Psalm 119:169, 173, 175, ESV

O, how Your collection of Hebrew poetry pillows my head in times of distress and heartache. Thank you for Your inspired music, penned to draw me to grace. Yahweh, You are my Song and my every reason to sing!

Day 193

Prepare a guest room for me, because I
hope to be restored to you in
answer to your prayers.
—PHILEMON V. 22, NIV

There are times in the day when the only music I hear is not music at all—it is a great, infinite forgiveness, an all comprehending love, a healing balm for a sick soul. It fills my soul with light and hope and peace like I am in a guestroom of heaven, and it passes all understanding.

≈

Day 194

Remember those who are in prison, as though
in prison with them, and those who are
mistreated, since you also are in the body.
—HEBREWS 13:3, ESV

Yes, Lord. Help me remember the mistreated, to feel for those imprisoned in pain, to love them. Let them lean their weary bodies on this very one You have created, and let us stagger on toward You, together, as one.

Day 195

We live close to death, but we are still alive.
We have been beaten, but we
have not been killed.
—2 CORINTHIANS 6:9

O, God Almighty, how You have saved me again and again. I have learned that with You by my side, I can be bruised but not beaten. And when my walk is slow, and my laughter is a cry, I am made happy by Your presence. What soul could want for more?

Day 196

Judge not, that you be not judged.
—MATTHEW 7:1, ESV

You are speaking directly to me, aren't you Lord? Yes, it seems almost ingrained in me to judge. Help me to remember this world is big enough for all kinds of people. In Your eyes there is no separation. We all matter equally. And what a blessed thing is that?

Day 197

The LORD is a jealous and avenging God
... Who can endure his fierce anger?
—NAHUM 1:2, 6, NIV

Lord, to know the full range of Your character is to recognize Your burning anger and jealousy as the flipside of Your love and mercy. You become angry with me because You love me! And Father, trust me, I know I grieve You and pray that by such awareness I progress the more swiftly!

≈

Day 198

He heals the brokenhearted and
bandages their wounds.
—PSALM 147:3

You call me to come as I am. You ask that I surrender my all. And so I do in my own broken-hearted way, watching the power of Your Love come down. You bandage up my wounds, kiss my soul, and I have nothing to offer, for I am Yours already. Will You take a heartfelt "thank you?"

Day 199

... do this in remembrance of me.
—1 Corinthians 11:24, ESV

It is just after sundown. The clouds lift and I see the crescent of the moon. You are about to die that I may be crowned with Your loving kindness and tender mercies. Your body breaks that I may be made whole. I beseech you, Lord, for words that would express how I feel. Perhaps silence most fits this day.

Day 200

... we suffer with Him, that we may
also be glorified together.
—Romans 8:17, NKJV

I fear that I'm too proud to suffer with others. I fear being too proud to speak to anyone when it comes to matters of my own pain or suffering, quite honestly. Therefore, I speak to You. And what do You—the grand Physician—say? "Lose your pride. Banish fear. Suffer and be glorified together." Ah, I see!

Day 201

The cloud of the Lord hovered over the Tabernacle
during the day, and at night fire glowed inside the
cloud so the whole family of Israel could see it.
—Exodus 40:38

*Lord, allow me confess all that I hide Open wide the windows of my
inner temple—the figurative tabernacle and innermost place of my
heart—that I may, without inhibition, welcome and invite the glory
of Your presence to inhabit every possible space within me.*

Day 202

... if another believer is overcome by some sin, you
who are godly should gently and humbly help that
person back onto the right path
—GALATIANS 6:1

*Relationships matter so much, is it any wonder broken relationships
threaten so! Lord, in handling frictions, let me not be void of Your
love and mercy. Pardon first my errors that I may not offend! Give
me light to restore things gently as I submit myself now to You with
humble trust.*

Day 203

Prepare for war! Rouse the warriors
... Let the weakling say, "I am strong!"
—JOEL 3:9, 10

*You speak to me in every event of my life, Father. You want to bless me,
but often I don't listen. I groan over this element in me. I chide it, and
attempt to make it bow. Help me, Lord! Awaken in me my need for
You, for without You I am weak; with You, I feel vibrant and strong.*

Day 204

I therefore, a prisoner for the Lord, urge you to
walk in a manner worthy of the calling to which
you have been called, with all humility and
gentleness, with patience, bearing
with one another in love …
—EPHESIANS 4:1–2, ESV

Lord, the call sounds simple: love me, love thy neighbor as thyself. But the strength it takes to peer deep within, accept our own pain, and welcome that of another is formidable. With Your help, it can be done. In fact, I can almost hear Your promised, "Well, done!"

Day 205

And because we are his children, God has sent
the Spirit of his Son into our hearts, prompting
us to call out, "Abba, Father."
—GALATIANS 4:6

Abba, I just want to make You proud of me today. Help me matter to just one person, Papa, please. Let me feel Your Spirit move deep inside of me, and let me respond in faithful obedience as Your child.

Day 206

Go and be reconciled to that person. Then
come and offer your sacrifice to God.
—MATTHEW 5:24

*O, Merciful Lord, how I desire reconciliation! This aching heart longs
for the bond which has been disunited to be reunited once more. Grant
me courage to convey this person's worth; risk all to regain their respect; and be ever-mindful of speaking love and grace. Bless this effort,
Lord! In all things, I give you thanks.*

≈

Day 207

PRAYER WALKING
He himself is the sacrifice that atones for our sins--
and not only our sins but the sins of all the world.
—1 JOHN 2:2

*Lord, may I bestow grace, love, and a special blessing on whomever
I come in contact with on my walk today—stranger or animal! Let
me taste selflessness, explore being outward-focused, and by this, let
others experience Your love—a love so supernatural they shall skip
with delight.*

Day 208

I will pour out my Spirit upon all people ... Your
old men will dream dreams, and your
young men will see visions.
—Joel 2:28

Lord, all too often I find myself in the heavens of my mind—ever distant yet so very real, so very intimately close. And though You tell me these things are not yet to be, You have given me a glimpse ... and that is enough to last me all my earthly days.

≈

Day 209

And what does the LORD require of you?
To act justly and to love mercy and to
walk humbly with your God.
—Micah 6:8, NIV

Who is like You, God? How do we become like You? Is it not by brushing up against one another in fellowship? Can I imitate the compassion I see in one, the modesty of another, the mercy of a third, and some other good virtue of a fourth? That is the answer, isn't it?

Day 210

If any of you wants to be my follower, you
must turn from your selfish ways, take up
your cross, and follow me.
—MATTHEW 16:24

Lord, Your spirit of self-sacrifice knows no limit. Is selflessness not the heart of worship? The love You showed, Jesus, drives every other virtue; it demands selflessness. It is the defining mark of a true disciple. May it define me!

Day 211

But you are a chosen people, a royal priesthood, a
holy nation, God's special possession, that you may
declare the praises of him who called you out of
darkness into his wonderful light.
—1 PETER 2:9, NIV

Evil battles good. Sorrow battles joy. Why would I wallow in darkness if I have been called into light? There is no power in darkness! Light strengthens; it soothes; it bathes everything in beauty, and beauty draws my attention to You! Yes, Lord, let me desire light over dark always!

Day 212

And so I will go to the king, which is against
the law; and if I perish, I perish!
—ESTHER 4:16, NKJV

*Beautiful, brave, and O, so loyal is a queen willing to die for her
cause—die to marriage, position, even to life itself. Esther was a
woman worthy of the title "queen." Inspire me, Lord. Create in me
such greatness.*

≈

Day 213

Don't be selfish; don't try to impress others. Be
humble, thinking of others as better than yourselves.
—PHILIPPIANS 2:3

*To the extent to which I can see myself through Your eyes, the less
self-absorbed I am in mine! Lord above, relinquish my selfishness that
I may enclose You, and the world around, in my arms. Eternal Love, it
is You I seek to impress, Your image I wish to reflect! Let the world be
inflamed with Thy love!*

Day 214

Then the LORD God said, "Behold, the man has
become like one of us in knowing good and evil."
—GENESIS 3:22, ESV

*Freedom to choose between good and evil is not freedom. No, for me,
Lord, freedom is being able to do the good that I want to do, but in
my corruptible mortal state, cannot. Freedom is being free to enjoy
the wondrous riches of your Grace. My liberator, my God, may I never forget it!*

≈

Day 215

Fight the good fight of faith ...
—1 TIMOTHY 6:12, NASB

*If faith by grace relieves this miserable soul, I shall fight to the death
before I let anyone rob me of it. I shall fight temptations of mind,
cravings, depression, hypocrisies, guilt, and I shall fight them with
the weapon of truth, empowered by You. Work in me, God, to will
and to do good.*

Day 216

Hold on to the pattern of wholesome
teaching you learned from me—a
pattern shaped by the faith and love
that you have in Christ Jesus.
—2 TIMOTHY 1:13

*Lord, how have I done? Have I guarded the faith? Have I passed
it along well? Are You as proud of me as Paul was of Timothy? Do
please say yes!*

≈

Day 217

So don't be anxious about tomorrow.
God will take care of your tomorrow
too. Live one day at a time.
—MATTHEW 6:34, TLB

*If I am anxious, I cannot possibly care for myself or for others. But
admonition to love myself and others seems only to increase anxiety!
Admonition doesn't make me love stronger; being in right relationship with You and others does! Help me do this. And Lord, please
know I am ever thankful for Your constant care!*

Day 218

God sent forth his Son ... to redeem those who
were under the law, that we might receive adoption
as sons. And because you are sons, God has sent
forth the Spirit of his Son into your hearts,
crying, "Abba! Father!"
—GALATIANS 4:1–6, NKJV

Who am I, but a member of Your community, Your family, and I am being enriched by fruits and gifts of the Holy Spirit. Is this not the moment of awareness I have sighed for? I cry out to You with praise: Abba, Father, You adopted me as yours—yours! Bless You forever and ever, amen.

Day 219

... greater is God's wonderful grace and his gift
of forgiveness to many through this
other man, Jesus Christ ...
—ROMANS 5:15

Lord, what makes faith in Christ profoundly different from the pro-found is forgiveness. You cure me through grace and provide a steady supply of forgiveness as oxygen to my soul. I can live as I know You have and will forgive me every single minute of every single day. How thankful I am!

Day 220

For God loved the world so much that he gave his one
and only Son, so that everyone who believes in
him will not perish but have eternal life.
—JOHN 3:16

My Majesty, your Son neither despised nor disowned any human be-ing. We must consider ourselves worthy for no other reason than that we are worthy to You. Yet how we struggle to grasp this! Awaken our hearts, Lord, that we may see mankind as You lovingly see!

≈

Day 221

Stand fast therefore in the liberty by which Christ
has made us free, and do not be entangled
again with a yoke of bondage.
—GALATIANS 5:1, NKJV

Use me to loosen the chains of souls held captive by false belief, legal-ism, pain, bitterness of spirit. In this sea of change, may people see individuals of strong resolve, trustworthiness, constancy of character. In the name of Jesus Christ, refine me, then send me to souls needing freedom in You!

Day 222

Have mercy on me, LORD, for I am faint; heal me,
LORD, for my bones are in agony.
—PSALM 6:2, NIV

O, Life of my Soul, who escapes torments of life, excruciating memories, enslavement to secrets, fears of being so bad as to be completely unlovable? God, I hate to admit the number of times I question if even You care. Have mercy on me, Lord. Heal me, for my agony is great!

Day 223

Beloved, do not be surprised at the fiery trial when
it comes upon you to test you, as though something
strange were happening to you. But rejoice insofar as
you share Christ's sufferings, that you may also rejoice
and be glad when his glory is revealed.
—1 PETER 4:12–13, ESV

You suffered so that we, who also suffer, might rise. Seeing Your glory, face-to-face, suffices me to know this pain will end, and the end is one glorious picture.

Day 224

... they finally discovered him in the Temple,
sitting among the religious teachers, listening
to them and asking questions.
—LUKE 2:46

Lord, I thank You for good memories and for great teachers—not the least of which was my own mother—gratitude made clearer in her absence. I echo her voice still, and am thankful to walk in the shadows of her faith. As I move into my day, it is with the hope that You alone be my Master and that study of Your Word preoccupies me always!

Day 225

Your love for one another will prove to the
world that you are my disciples.
—JOHN 13:35

For Your name sake, Lord, recover broken fellowship the world over. People matter, and our reputation as your people matters! Let nothing divert attention from You. In all things, let us strive to praise and adore You. I thank You, and pray for continued help in forging wonderful ties this side of Heaven.

Day 226

He is before all things, and in him
all things hold together.
—COLOSSIANS 1:17, NIV

What force are You if not unifying? Do You not hold the universe together? Is it not You who holds me together?! Yet I am made after You. Should I not be a force for unity, too?

≈

Day 227

I was born and came into the world to testify
to the truth. All who love the truth
recognize that what I say is true.
—JOHN 18:37

If I love the truth, why do I seek to conceal things, embellish, or fictionalize them? Do forgive me for this, Lord! Difficult as it is to speak words of truth, bitter or sweet, You assure me that I can do all things with Your power and grace. And for that, I bless Thy holy name!

Day 228

Above all, keep loving one another earnestly,
since love covers a multitude of sins.
—1 PETER 4:8–10

How magnificent is your love, O, Lord! Shallow, superficial love doesn't cover over mistakes—fervent, intentional, earnest love does—Your love blankets our sins, and how desperate I am to love like You do! I yearn to, Father. Show me how that I may warm the hearts of others as You have mine. Thank you, Lord, thank you!

Day 229

Sing for joy, O heavens! Rejoice, O earth! Burst
into song, O mountains! For the LORD has
comforted his people and will have
compassion on them in their suffering.
—Isaiah 49:13

Let us not underestimate how hard it is to be compassionate … it requires the inner disposition to go with others to a place where they are weak, vulnerable, lonely, and broken. But this is not our spontaneous response to suffering. What we desire most is to do away with suffering by fleeing from it or finding a quick cure for it.
—HENRI NOUWEN IN *THE WAY OF THE HEART*

Day 230

Rejoice in the Lord always;
again I will say, rejoice.
—PHILIPPIANS 4:4, ESV

My God of Gods, how I would do everything in my truth-laden power to keep joy ever-present in sorrow and suffering! I supplicate You for ongoing miracles and fresh ones for those who have never tasted them. Come down, Lord, and do Your deepest work as we rejoice You always!

Day 231

He himself bore our sins in his body on the tree,
that we might die to sin and live to righteousness.
By his wounds you have been healed.
—1 PETER 2:24, ESV

My wounds don't feel so healed, nor does my head nor heart, but I perceive You to feel what I feel, and take comfort in that. Lord, You took on every human experience that through You we may ascend this life. Are there words that capture the magnitude of that beyond "thank you"?

Day 232

The LORD will fight for you;
you need only to be still.
—Exodus 14:14, NIV

*When my back's against the wall, and my strength completely gone, this
is when You move in closer and hold me up. I need not fight. I needn't
utter a single word. I need only to be still. Nonetheless, thank you.*

Day 233

JAHWEH, LORD ABOVE ALL
... the people returned to ways even more corrupt
than those of their ancestors, following other gods
and serving and worshiping them. They refused to
give up their evil practices and stubborn ways.
—JUDGES 2:19, NIV

*What happens when we run from You, when we underestimate evil
powers, and when we settle for anything or anyone less than You?
Bluntly put, we fail. We self-defeat. Why, Lord? Why do I find myself in endless plight? Reveal my stubborn ways! Uproot them! Let
me change . . .*

Day 234

And they were singing the song of Moses,
the servant of God, and the song of the Lamb:
"Great and marvelous are your works ..."
—REVELATION 15:3

*Lord, it is in worship of you that full expressions of spirituality unfold,
from confession to repentance, forgiveness to acceptance, responsibility to privilege. As a lotus of numerous petals that bless and inspire,
delight and free, so let my voice of praise glorify thee!*

Day 235

... to another faith by the same Spirit, to another
gifts of healing by the one Spirit ...
—1 Corinthians 12:9, ESV

Differentness can bind us together or tear us apart. When the latter occurs, I can only pray for Your presence to be made known, for I have come to expect marvelous things when You arrive. You never disappoint. For this reason alone, I am able to embrace differences in human nature; moreover, find reason to celebrate them!

Day 236

But in all things we commend ourselves as
ministers of God: in much patience, in
tribulations, in needs, in distresses ...
—2 Corinthians 6:4, NKJV

Is it not in happily knowing You and being known by You IN sorrow and sufferings that I show You to be real? Yes, for Thou art the cause of my joy! In the shadowy midst of reality—in pain, in loss—I confess Your confidence to the world. May they see me blossom into light!

Day 237

Let us also lay aside every weight, and sin which
clings so closely, and let us run with endurance
the race that is set before us, looking to Jesus, the
founder and perfecter of our faith … and is seated
at the right hand of the throne of God.
—HEBREWS 12:1–2, ESV

*Strip me bare, Lord. Cast away that which weighs me down! And let
me run free this race with eyes ever on You—my eternal prize.*

≈

Day 238

… what manner of persons ought you to be
in holy conduct and godliness …
—2 PETER 3:11, NKJV

*What I do and how I do it matters, but why I do what I ought to do
should set me apart. Lord, help me consciously choose to act in love;
to live my whole life, and further, to be willing to lay down my life, in
obedience to an inward condition of love. Out of love for You, I pray.*

Day 239

... we will speak the truth in love, growing in
every way more and more like Christ ...
—EPHESIANS 4: 15

Lord, I seek Your grace in bringing matters into the light. Permit me to speak gently yet truthfully; always with the intent of becoming more like Christ. Enlighten me to make good on times when love is tried that I may serve my brother well, and by this, let me find favour in Your eyes.

Day 240

... let God transform you into a new person
by changing the way you think.
—ROMANS 12:2

Lord, You have transformed my entire being, broken through the prison doors of my pain, revealed my anguish, and have granted me grace to speak of it! Thank you for caring enough to burst through these walls and enter my suffering. That You lift me out of it day after day is cause for praise, so thank you, my God, thank you!

Day 241

But you will receive power when the
Holy Spirit comes upon you.
—ACTS 1:8

Can there be a more action-packed book than Acts? I have always loved it best, for it communicates life through the Spirit—boldly, magnificently, grandly! I love how the book leaves me hanging … it cannot finish, as the story is unfinished! What then, Lord, is my part? And how does it thus end?

≈

Day 242

The aim of our charge is love that issues from a pure
heart and a good conscience and a sincere faith.
—1 TIMOTHY 1:5, ESV

Lord let me gain a tighter grasp on faith by grace. I know it should free this heart from all that hinders it in love: free it from the effects of guilt; from the hypocrisy of covering over guilt; from the fear of being found guilty—is it any wonder faith is one giant leap? Gift it to me, please!

Day 243

The pride of your heart has deceived you, you who
live in the clefts of the rocks and make your home
on the heights, you who say to yourself, 'Who
can bring me down to the ground?'
—OBADIAH v. 3, NIV

*O, let not pride deceive me, trick me, trap me, ensnare me! Woe am I if
I think I'm invincible, or cannot fall. Rather let the Spirit rule my flesh
that victorious I will be!*

≈

Day 244

But exhort one another every day, as long as
it is called "today," that none of you may be
hardened by the deceitfulness of sin.
—HEBREWS 3:13, ESV

*Soften my heart, O gracious God. I have sinned behind Your back and
in front of Your face. Yes, if there was ever a hypocrite, it was me. Forgive me, Lord. See my remorse and hasten the day that sin and death
are swallowed up forever!*

Day 245

If he listens to you, you have gained your brother.
—MATTHEW 18:15, ESV

If I need to speak into another's life, Lord, will You remind me to begin with listening? With listening comes understanding; with understanding, comes respect; with respect, love. Let us counsel with the intent of striving and thriving together, as one community, as one nation, as one globe. May Your peace be ours.

≈

Day 246

We realize that we have sinned, but
now we are ready to enter the land the
LORD has promised us.
—NUMBERS 14:40

Lord, it is a dangerous land this. Fear and anxiety tower like fiercesome giants, but when You are here I'm not afraid. I can tell others what it is like, what I have seen, heard and touched, and encourage them to enter their own promised but dangerous places in stride. You are with us as promised. Amen.

Day 247

O LORD, you have examined my heart
and know everything about me.
—PSALM 139:1

You know me most of all, Lord. You made me! So permit me honest self-examination. Let me deny my fallen self, and then set me on the road to self-discovery, for how wondrous it would be to radiate Your light more brightly!

≈

Day 248

I remember your genuine faith ... I
remind you to fan into flames the
spiritual gift God gave you...
—2 TIMOTHY 1:5–7

How comely is the child-like faith of Timothy's! Why is it, Lord, that the more I grow in knowledge, the harder it is to remain humble and innocent in spirit? Oh how often I see that the most gifted are the least aware of their spiritual gifts. Lord, let me be humble, please.

Day 249

When Jesus had finished saying these things, the
crowds were amazed at his teaching.
—MATTHEW 7:28

*How would You choose to communicate to people today? Through the
pulpit, ladies' Bible study groups, men's golf retreats, Bible colleges or
seminaries, or through the mediums of social media, television, and
printed page? Would I scoff or be amazed by Your teaching? Would I
know the difference?*

Day 250

And you must love the Lord your God with all
your heart, all your soul, all your mind, and all
your strength.' The second is equally important:
'Love your neighbor as yourself.'
—MARK 12:30–31

*I have a fearless desire to love You, my God. I have an almost self-
less desire to love my neighbour; but virtually no desire to love myself.
May I remember today that I am made in Your image, and thus am
worthy, deserving of love. I beg Thee, please.*

Day 251

... the wisdom we speak of is
the mystery of God ...
—1 CORINTHIANS 2:7

Deeper than our craving for possessions, prestige, social power, or sexual potency is our craving for knowledge of the end and beginning of life. Christ gives us that knowledge—knowledge that satisfies the human mind and spirit—knowledge that produced good fruit!

≈

Day 252

We faithfully preach the truth. God's power
is working in us. We use the weapons of
righteousness in the right hand for
attack and the left hand for defense.
—2 CORINTHIANS 6:7

From whence and whither comes powerful joy in the midst of life's battles? Is it not from Your Word that I absorb joy, strong and unshakeable as rock under my feet? O, God of the impossible, let them see that my strength comes from Thee, especially in the midst of suffering!

Day 253

We are the clay, and You our potter;
And all we are the work of Your hand.
—ISAIAH 64:8, NKJV

Am I prepared to walk through fire for You, my grand Creator? Am I willing to have my soul tested, my character refined, my vessel beautified by braving the darkness and weathering the fires of persecution? O Lord, give me courage as You complete Your work in me!

Day 254

But I lavish unfailing love for a thousand
generations on those who love me and
obey my commands.
—EXODUS 20:6

O, Father, how I rejoice in Your Word! Thank you for allowing me to meditate and reflect upon each nugget read willingly, without compulsion. Please nourish my longing for You, and grant me opportunities to honour You well. And thank you, Lord, for lavishing me with Your unfailing love.

Day 255

... he changed his mind and did not carry out the
destruction he had threatened.
—JONAH 3:10

*We care about ourselves, our needs, our paltry things, but You, You
care about people—real, living, anxiety-plagued people. O, merciful
God, turn not my face from those swallowed up by guilt or depression,
but use me. Let them derive consolation from the words You impart,
just as I derive courage from You to stay the course!*

≈

Day 256

God Himself will be with them and be their God.
And God will wipe away every tear from their eyes;
there shall be no more death, nor sorrow, nor
crying. There shall be no more pain, for the
former things have passed away.
—REVELATION 21:3–4, NKJV

*Lord, if there is anyone who can see joy in my sorrow, and sorrow in
my joy, it is You. I thank You for giving my mind's eye a glimpse of
suffering washed away, and for filling my heart with a mighty song, I
praise You always.*

Day 257

If possible, so far as it depends on you,
be at peace with all men.
—ROMANS 12:18, NASB

To be peaceable I must have peace. And any recipe for peace demands emptying myself out, flushing away all the debris that clouds my inner seas, and then, asking You to pour ample portions of your calming Spirit in. Let me think about that for a moment. Yes, I do believe it's worth a try!

≈

Day 258

Let us think of ways to motivate one another
to acts of love and good works.
—HEBREWS 10:24

O, how daily stresses take their toll! But what a simple word of encouragement does to the spiritually depleted soul. It lift us up, refuels our spirit, and incites us to greater acts of love yet. Lord, please let me do this for one person today. You know who they are. Bring them to me.

Day 259

Go in peace and be freed
from your suffering.
—MARK 5:34, NIV

It is time, my confidante, to bow before You and confess my need for your healing touch. Open my life to Your touch in the whisper of the wind and in the crack of thunder, in the warmth of the sun, the pull of the moon, and in the loud beating of my heart. Free me from my suffering, please!

≈

Day 260

Draw near to God, and He
will draw near to you.
—JAMES 4:8, ESV

You offer life abundant; promise obedient ones protection and blessing; and have written the most beautiful love letter in the whole wide world. Indeed, a more attractive invitation I have yet to receive. And what do You ask of me other than to open it and respond?

Day 261

Then the Pharisees called a meeting
to plot how to kill Jesus.
—MATTHEW 12:14

Would we hail You for slicing through the maze of theological dogma, exposing political and social oppression, cracking the illusion of man-made peace and security? Would we appoint You governor or denounce You as traitor? Would my eyes look upon You with suspicion or trust?

Day 262

When I saw him, I fell at his feet as though dead.
But he laid his right hand on me, saying,
"Fear not, I am the first and the last ..."
—REVELATION 1:17, ESV

I fall down before You with deep reverence and awe. This sinful heart! This miserable soul! How can You look upon me with grace? I beg that You render me whole before You; render me forgiven as I bow before Your merciful throne today.

≈

Day 263

I tell you the truth, when you did it to one of the
least of these my brothers and sisters,
you were doing it to me!
—MATTHEW 25:40

Lord, may the compassion of Your Son be made visible in my world through me. May I learn to see people as Your Son would see them and love them, without disparity, for we are all human beings—all of us stand as equals before Your throne—and, all of us are in desperate need of You!

Day 264

Oh, how great are God's riches
and wisdom and knowledge!
—ROMANS 11:33

Lord, one of the surest way to strengthen human bonds is to think and speak highly of the person at hand. David spent many a starry night gazing upon celestial skies declaring You a marvelously incomparable Creator. It is my intent today, Father, to laud You likewise, but I am forgetful—so please grant this request!

≈

Day 265

He has made everything beautiful in its time.
He has also set eternity in the human heart;
yet no one can fathom what God has
done from beginning to end.
—ECCLESIASTES 3:11, NIV

Is it any wonder momentary explanations fail? Deeper into the meaning of life, into the soul, into your Godship, do I look, for You made me to hunger for eternal truth. Only in the direction of You shall I find reason for existence and for my heart to love as it has the notion and power to.

Day 266

You will be hated by all for my name's sake.
But not a hair of your head will perish.
—Luke 21:17–18, ESV

Sacrificial living carries promise of protection. All my life, Lord, I have walked with angels on either side of the road. When I grieved, they comforted. Where I was burdened, they lightened. And in each one, I saw You. Where I am You are, and I know You will protect me forevermore.

≈

Day 267

... count it all joy when you fall
into various trials ...
—James 1:2, NKJV

Lord, even when ill, when suffering hits, when weaknesses abound, I can get up in the morning and thank You, work, break off, thank You, and then sleep. In a way, You enable me to live despite sadness in blessed enchantment, day in and day out. However can I thank You?

Day 268

Be anxious for nothing, but in everything by prayer
and supplication with thanksgiving let your
requests be made known to God.
—Philippians 4:6, NASB

*I am hearing the need to discern Your voice. Accept my faults. Decide
and commit to act. Then, pray hard! You desire to remedy my mis-
chief, strangely. Do You pray for me also?*

≈

Day 269

The things you have learned and received and
heard and seen in me, practice these things,
and the God of peace will be with you.
—Philippians 4:9, NASB

*O, that I shall let conflict showcase Your goodness at work! In the
mirror of others, shall I see ways to better please and glorify You. Shall
this troublesome soul suffer from ruined relations, but seek to rectify
them at once? I shall, Lord, to the glory of You, the great God of peace,
forevermore.*

Day 270

Stand up and praise the Lord your God, for he
lives from everlasting to everlasting.
—NEHEMIAH 9:5

O, how these words stir! So often accomplishments overshadow spiritual needs. Let me be like the people of Nehemiah's day; complete my work swiftly and make time for celebration—listening to You, praising You from daybreak to midday. Indeed, why wait? Lord, let me lift Your name on high!

Day 271

... preach the word; be ready in season and out
of season; reprove, rebuke, and exhort, with
complete patience and teaching.
—2 TIMOTHY 4:2, ESV

You have blessed my body and mind with refreshment, dear Father, now let me give them back to You as an entire sacrifice. With humble thanks, I shall go out unto the world, not faintly, but with courage and cheerfulness. Praised be Your name for all time!

Day 272

The sinful nature wants to do evil, which is just the
opposite of what the Spirit wants. And the Spirit
gives us desires that are the opposite of what
the sinful nature desires. These two forces are
constantly fighting each other, so you are
not free to carry out your good intentions.
—GALATIANS 5:17

*Lord, you sent Your Son not to redeem but to destroy fallen human-
ness. Let me be vigilant in dying to that side of my fallen self that I
may begin to live!*

≈

Day 273

You are my dearly loved Son, and
you bring me great joy.
—LUKE 3:22

*Being in Christ's presence must feel like standing in the sun. How
much joy He brings! How His disciples lived for their happy times together. Did He not accept them, affirm them, love them, rejoice them,
bond with them in affection and esteem? Dare I confess my feelings
mirror His?*

Day 274

Either way, Christ's love controls us.
—2 Corinthians 5:14

So strangely perfect was Christ's perfectness. He notices all I fail to; erases all the smudges of ego I fall prey to; fills all the needs I ignore; dismantles all the barriers I erect. He empties His entire being out in my behalf! So complete is His love, I am made complete in turn.

≈

Day 275

I pray that you may enjoy good health ... even
as your soul is getting along well ... continue
to walk in it [the truth] ... [for] you are
faithful in what you are doing for the
brothers ... do not imitate what is
evil but what is good. Peace to you.
—3 John vv. 2–14, NIV

Be strong of soul. Walk by truth. Faithfully give. Imitate goodness. And peace will be mine? Yes, mine! For these rhythms of life, I thank Thee!

Day 276

Create in me a pure heart, O God, and
renew a steadfast spirit within me.
—PSALM 51:10, NIV

*When another speaks truth into my life, Lord, let me accept it. Let me
prove willing to change. How I pray for You to create in me a heart like
Your own! Be in me, with me. Act in me. Chastise me. Make me grow.
I trust You, Father. I have seen what You can do. Develop me, please!*

Day 277

Many shall be purified, made
white, and refined ...
—DANIEL 12:10, NKJV

*I pray that when You look upon me it is through the filtered lens of
the blood of the Lamb. Do wash my conscience clean. Purify the intentions of my heart! Make white my soul. And set my countenance
aglow with bountiful love for Thee!*

Day 278

Have this mind among yourselves,
which is yours in Christ Jesus ...
—PHILIPPIANS 2:5, ESV

Lord, you affirm me to be a child of Yours, a member of Christ, an heir to the throne, but the most vital gift of all is a picture of what I can become in Christ! You accept me already for what I can become in Christ. What more can this weeping heart ask?

≈

Day 279

... worship in spirit and truth.
—JOHN 4:24, ESV

How is it possible for me to worship You rightly if I am at odds with my brother? What part do I have in agreeing or disagreeing in love? Can I encourage the art of speaking truth-in-love in my home, in my community? How it must sadden You when trifles cost fellowship! Let not another offense hinder my offering of praise to You. Be glorified, my Father, forever and ever! Amen.

Day 280

Therefore be imitators of God,
as beloved children.
—EPHESIANS 5:1, ESV

You are my tutor, my guide, my father. Why would I, Your child, not want to imitate everything she sees her magnificent Papa do? I worship You! I adore You! I am charmed by You. My heart laments that I cannot emulate Your virtue more fully. Let me please!

≈

Day 281

When he saw Jesus from a distance, he ran and fell
on his knees in front of him. He shouted at the
top of his voice, "What do you want with
me, Jesus, Son of the Most High God?"
—MARK 5:6–7, NIV

Ah! You desire that I seek You out, fall on my knees and pour my miseries out, don't You, Lord? Well, if healing involves admission, let me admit my needs that You may come down from on high, meet me where I am, and minister to me!

Day 282

By sending his own Son in the likeness
of sinful flesh and for sin, he
condemned sin in the flesh...
—ROMANS 8:3, ESV

This sinful this flesh, these wrongful desires, how do You look upon me and not cringe, O Holy One? Am I to believe, truly believe, that You clothed Your own son, Your first-born, in the likeness of my sinful flesh that my guilt should be stripped away? Do persuade me this is so!

Day 283

And even when you saw this happening, you
refused to believe him and repent of your sins.
—MATTHEW 21:32

If you were to come back today, would I seek Your vim and vigour, wit and warmth, passion and power, and authoritative action? Would I see a blazing figure with a face "like the sun shining in all its brilliance," or see a "normal" man? Would I be disappointed or pleased with the real You?

Day 284

O Father, Lord of heaven and earth, thank you
for hiding these things from those who think
themselves wise and clever, and for
revealing them to the childlike.
—MATTHEW 11:25

If You returned without pomp and fanfare, without title and office, without vestments and priestly garb, would we cast You out, abandon and deny You as God-sent? Tell me, would we cheat, conspire, compete to extinguish your light? Would I, Your servant, see Your spirit within?

Day 285

When the crowds heard him, they were
astounded at his teaching.
—MATTHEW 22:33

Even beyond the doing of good, was the impact had by Christ's teachings! O, how He spoke! How often, yet how incorrectly, I assume dark clouds withhold sunshine from the unjust. But not You; You tell me the sun rises and sets on all. What a wind of freedom His teachings bring!

Day 286

"Tell the truth to each other. Stop your love of
telling lies that you swear are the truth.
I hate all these things," says the Lord.
—ZECHARIAH 8:17

*As I speak into the lives of others with "truth in love," may I invite
them to speak truth into mine! Father, let your love excite us toward
implementing a language of caring in this world. O, what a difference
it would make! Indeed, grant us wisdom to make this a reality.*

Day 287

Now faith is the assurance of things hoped for,
the conviction of things not seen.
—HEBREWS 11:1, ESV

*I am bound by belief in You; trust You implicitly; and though I have
never seen You, have felt Your love. With eyes wide open, I place my
complete and utter faith in You. I confess that You are more to me
than all the rest of the world, and am as certain of You, today, as I
ever have been!*

Day 288

The human heart is the most deceitful of
all things, and desperately wicked.
Who really knows how bad it is?
—Jeremiah 17:9, ESV

*You know me through and through. You have inhabited my soul,
permeated my mind, possessed me entirely; You seem to rejoice in all
my ways—my idiosyncrasies and peculiarities, my longings and life
rhythms. You alone know my heart, and still, You love me. Why, O
why, shan't I?*

≈

Day 289

Do not neglect to show hospitality to strangers, for
thereby some have entertained angels unawares.
—Hebrews 13:2, ESV

*Have I entertained an angel today? Is this why the flame within my
broken heart glows like an opal? Is this what hospitality calls us to?
To light the taper of each other's souls with loving kindness? O that I
make intentional space for others to come in, Lord. And may I think
upon You always.*

Day 290

Iron sharpens iron, and one
man sharpens another.
—PROVERBS 27:17, ESV

Lord keep me from the error of thinking I can go along. Teach me humility. Show me the joy of thinking, hoping, praying, and walking together as people set aside for You. Wipe away my foolish pride. Let my skills be sharpened upon the whet-stone of lessons learned through shared living. In Christ's name, I pray. Amen.

≈

Day 291

But when I hoped for good, evil came,
and when I waited for light, darkness came.
—JOB 30:26, ESV

I am dark and light, beautiful and ugly, shameful and proud, good and evil. O, omniscient God, which power shall win out today? Recall my wiser sense! Rekindle my affections for truth and love, goodness and honor! Give me strength to grow from child to daughter that I may honour You always.

Day 292

In that day I will restore the fallen house of David. I
will repair its damaged walls. From the ruins I
will rebuild it and restore its former glory.
—Amos 9:11

My God, would You weave some order through the chaos I've cre-
ated? Guide me in the light of faith to mend and repair, and not
to isolate myself. Father, I'd sooner perish than isolate myself from
You! I need You, Lord. Help me restore these ruined relations to their
former glory. Amen.

Day 293

... all life would cease, and humanity
would turn again to dust.
—Job 34:15

We are, because we have been made. The earth is, because it has been made. Creatures are, because they have been made. We are utterly connected; all dependent upon the earth; and like all created beings, utterly dependent on You for sustenance! Let us hold the earth dear, till it, and keep it. Just as You asked, so may it be!

Day 294

I am the way, the truth,
and the life.
—John 14:6

O, God eternal, You are the personification of love! All Your ways are true! How desirous this cowardly soul is for You to make brave her speech today! May Your exquisite love sweeten my proclivity for truth that I shall more closely resemble Your essence. Make me more like You!

Day 295

Follow me now. Let the spiritually
dead bury their own dead.
—MATTHEW 8:22

I wonder, would I be among the mighty throng, small remnant, or perhaps just the two or three who, at the return of Christ's presence, is moved beyond measure to commit my life to His ideals? What extent would I go to, what cost would I pay, to forsake all and follow Him right now?

≈

Day 296

I am insignificant and despised, but I
don't forget your commandments.
—PSALM 119:141

Some days it takes every ounce of power to muster up the strength to love—every ounce of power. But even in the midst of self-loathing, I am asked to obey. And with obedience comes blessings, and from blessings, insurmountable joy. I love You, dear Father.

Day 297

Arise, Jerusalem! Let your light shine for all to see.
For the glory of the LORD rises to shine on you.
—ISAIAH 60:1

O God, whose boundless love and joy
are present everywhere,
He cannot come to visit you
unless you are not there.
—ANGELUS SILESIUS

Lord, let the boundless love and joy that shone through Jesus life shine
ever brightly in me!

≈

Day 298

The spirit indeed is willing, but the flesh is weak.
—MATTHEW 26:41, ESV

It is well past midnight as I travel the narrow streets of Jerusalem with
you. The day was long; my soul, fatigued. It is even hard to pray. But
you, You Lord, are gracious and ever so kind. "It's alright," You say.
"Your flesh is weak, but your spirit strong. Still, I know you can do
this, my child."

Day 299

When he saw Jesus from a distance, he ran
and fell on his knees in front of him.
—MARK 5:6, NIV

Suffering separates me from the rest of the world, Father. The pain is too great to share, and thus I feel constantly on the outside looking in. Rare are the souls that companion one so frantic in spirit with sorrow. Send just one Lord, I beg Thee!

Day 300

Thunder roared and lightning flashed, and a dense
cloud came down on the mountain …and all
the people trembled … All of Mount Sinai
was covered with smoke because the Lord
had descended on it in the form of fire.
—EXODUS 19:16–18

Lord, thank you for daily discoveries and revelations and for Moses-like moments: those trembling, quivering, prayerful moments on bended knee as well as the soul-enchanted, heart-inflamed moments of joy found in Your unveiled glory!

Day 301

Jesus looked at them and said, "With man this is
impossible, but with God all things are possible."
—MATTHEW 19:26, NIV

*When joy seems fleeting, Lord, I trust You hear the songs I cannot
sing. When I am ashamed and filled with remorse, I pray that Your
eyes look upon me with hope. When the enthusiasm in my heart
wanes, grant me new dreams and new visions. Make me whole, if only
in spirit!*

≈

Day 302

What is man, that he can be pure? Or he who is
born of a woman, that he can be righteous?
—JOB 15:14

*What is man? What is woman? What is thy self? Are we not the most
complex beings of all, dear God? Neither all good nor all evil, nor entirely shameful nor entirely glorious, but a wildly diverse combination
of all these things? Instruct me, Lord, that I may know!*

Day 303

If you do this thing and God so commands you,
then you will be able to endure ...
—Exodus 18:23, NASB

If I seek to accomplish things on my own, chances are I'll fail. But if You have commanded it, if it coincides with Your will, then how I can fail? For surely You are with me!

≈

Day 304

He [God] disarmed the rulers and authorities and put
them to open shame, by triumphing over them in him.
—Colossians 2:15, ESV

You, my triumphant defender, are stronger than all of them—stronger than Satan and his legion. And You disarmed the one weapon Satan had over me: the weapon of unforgiven sin; snatched it from his hands, punished it, nailed it to the cross, gone! Is it any wonder I am ingratiated to Thee?

Day 305

They sought God eagerly, and he was found by them.
So the LORD gave them rest on every side.
—2 CHRONICLES 15:15, NIV

I sought after You, my King. O, how I sought after You! And what did I find? Rest. I found nothing is comparable to Your authority. All else is "a chasing after the wind." Your principles are eternal; graceful yet just, like cushions of cotton clouds hung aloft to rest my eye on grandiose immensity!

≈

Day 306

Don't be afraid; just believe.
—MARK 5:36, NIV

Lord, so afraid was I in my brokenness that You would leave me. Now I know that You cannot leave me, for I am Your creation, Your child, Your purpose, Your love. You believe in me as I believe in You. When I cry out for peace, it is You that arrives. Yes, You are the "peace" I seek!

Day 307

FIXED HOUR PRAYER
For the angel of the LORD is a guard; he
surrounds and defends all who fear him.
—PSALM 34:7

Lord, I thank you for my precious, precious children. May the gift of prayer and praise, reading of scripture, petition-making sustain their spirit throughout their every day, their every night, and in all the years to come. And Lord, may they never, for a single minute, not feel the extravagance of your love.

Day 308

All humanity finds shelter in the
shadow of your wings.
—PSALM 36:7

Have we witnessed as overwhelming a love for humanity as Christ's? O that I would accept that love and have it flow through me with tidal waves of passion! Let the infinity of Your love pierce the core of my being and prompt one response alone: gratitude for the wonders of Your grace!

Day 309

Then everyone will see the Son of
Man coming on the clouds with
great power and glory.
—MARK 13:26

Some say that ever 'gainst that season comes
Wherein our Savior's birth is celebrated,
The bird of dawning singeth all night long;
And then, they say, no spirit can walk abroad;
The nights are wholesome; then no planets strike,
No fairy tales, or witch hath power to charm,
So hallow'd and so gracious is the time.
—Shakespeare (*Hamlet*, I.i.157-163)

Privileged us mortals are now to see You through a mirror darkly, but
soon shall we behold Your glory, in all its dazzling brilliance, face to
face! To that end, let us press on ever boldly to the end. To Your name
be the glory, amen.

Day 310

Then I acknowledged my sin to you and did not
cover up my iniquity. I said, "I will confess my
transgressions to the LORD." And you
forgave the guilt of my sin.
—PSALM 32:5, NIV

*Father, unveil my iniquities. Open this heart to hearing from You even
in the unlikeliest of places. I need not ask long or cry loud, for quickly
You do reveal, and always are You near.*

Day 311

Fear of the LORD is the foundation of
true knowledge, but fools despise
wisdom and discipline.
—PROVERBS 1:7

*Almost every thought within me is brought into harmony with the
Proverbs, and what few thoughts are not brought into harmony are
brought into subjection by them. You have appointed my conscience,
heart, and mind, as faithful guides within my whole self. Thank you!
O that they remain in Your charge.*

Day 312

Remember the word that I said to you: 'A servant
is not greater than his master.' If they persecuted
me, they will also persecute you.
—JOHN 15:20, ESV

*Where there is passion for Christ, there is persecution. My scars have
their own sad stories to tell. But then again, what good are tearless
hearts for healing wounds? What good is a life lived safely for self?
Rather, let my afflictions comfort others and herald You, my Lord!*

Day 313

The blessing of the LORD makes a person
rich, and he adds no sorrow with it.
—PROVERBS 10:22

*Trust takes work, Father. But I know that if I meditate on Your works
past, present, and future, my trust in You shall be all the more unbreakable; and the more I trust, the more I shall praise and honour
You. That is what makes one rich, spiritually rich, my Father, and
THAT is a blessing galore!*

Day 314

He trains my hands for battle; he strengthens
my arm to draw a bronze bow.
—PSALM 18:34

Lord, You can do anything You wish. You can make the heavens pour down rain on dry lands; You can soften the snow on ice-capped mountains until rivers joyously flow; You can command the winds to carry away the burdens of this Earth; and You can strengthen me.

≈

Day 315

And the peace of God, which surpasses all
understanding, will guard your hearts
and your minds in Christ Jesus.
—PHILIPPIANS 4:7, ESV

Let me encounter Your Spirit at home with myself, in my deepest, most profound inner sanctuary, that when turbulence hits, I may ride the storm with courage and grace. I will recognize and embrace the protective winds of Your Holy Spirit enveloping me with peace and tranquility.

Day 316

You answer us with awesome and righteous deeds,
God our Savior, the hope of all the ends of the
earth and of the farthest seas...
—PSALM 65:5, NIV

Who gains a following based on a message of faith, love, and hope?
Who has the courage to cut through the murky waters of religious
apathy and start a revolt? Who, but Christ, has the power to work
miracles? Who yet can move and change and stir the hearts and souls
of men, but You?

Day 317

God is faithful, and he will not let you be tempted
beyond your ability, but with the temptation he
will also provide the way of escape, that
you may be able to endure it.
—1 CORINTHIANS 10:13, ESV

In the deepest, darkest prisons of pain, when I beg for release and fear
it shall not come, suddenly You appear—and in Your presence I see the
light of day; I see the way out. And there is always another way out.

Day 318

This is the way; walk in it.
—Isaiah 30:21, NIV

Do I hear a "word behind me" telling me which way to go? Do I hear Your Spirit speak, hear You through Your Word, hear You in the voice of Your people? Father, open my heart, my ears, my eyes, my closed fists! Let me hear beyond what I am willing to hear that I shall not miss the voice behind me showing me the way!

≈

Day 319

I will rejoice in doing them good . . .
—Jeremiah 32:41, NIV

What a moving epitaph it is to be known simply for doing good! O, how this soul vibrates with wonder at Christ's actions! Without affectations, He went about uplifting, counselling, helping the ordinary, the extraordinary, and the unlikely! If divine goodness exists, is THIS not how it behaves?

Day 320

For the Father loves the Son and shows
him everything he is doing.
— JOHN 5:20

To make sense of Christ's admonitions is to see them in the light of Your absolute and unconditional love. Give the shirt off your back. Go the extra mile. Why? Because You have given far more and have gone far longer stretches! Truly, how extravagant is Your love!

≈

Day 321

For the Mighty One is holy, and he has
done great things for me… For he made
this promise to our ancestors, to
Abraham and his children forever.
—LUKE 1:49, 55

Though filled with confusion and fear, Mary says "yes" to Your invitation, regardless of personal cost. Is it any wonder she is held by many to be Your first and dearest disciple?

Day 322

We believe that we are all saved the same way,
by the undeserved grace of the Lord Jesus.
—ACTS 15:11

Lord, I am alive by Your grace. I am saved by Your grace. My fragilities and frailties, my anxieties and angers, my petulance and peculiarities are saved by Your grace. I can love myself, and thus, love others, because of Your grace! Thank you. Thank you. Thank you.

Day 323

Anyone who claims to know all the answers doesn't
really know very much. But the person who loves
God is the one whom God recognizes.
—1 CORINTHIANS 8:2–3

Spare me from thinking I know anything at all about love. You took upon Yourself to break through our barriers—OUR barriers, making visible the suffering of Your Son, pleading our case, selflessly. When I think I have loved like You, I discover that I have not loved as I ought. Teach me, Lord, please!

Day 324

And we urge you, brothers, admonish the idle,
encourage the fainthearted, help the
weak, be patient with them all.
—1 Thessalonians 5:14, ESV

Be patient with me, Lord, I beg You to. I admonish more than I encourage, and I lean towards impatience with Your people. You are so kind, so gentle, so long-suffering, so good. Teach me to be. And thank you for putting up with this faint-hearted soul daily!

≈

Day 325

Above all, clothe yourselves with love, which
binds us all together in perfect harmony.
—Colossians 3:14

O, don't the little things make a big difference in how we love one another? Truly, it is the countless smaller acts—a warm hug, a kind remark, a thoughtful gesture, a knowing smile that bind us together in love and harmony, that makes life worth the living, that reflects a healthy relationship with You. Lest I forget this!

Day 326

Again, the kingdom of heaven is like treasure hidden
in a field, which a man found and hid; and for joy over
it he goes and sells all that he has and buys that field.
—MATTHEW 13:44, NKJV

*If my faith is secure enough, shouldn't it be pushing the greed in my
heart aside? If dwelling in Your Kingdom, Lord, is what makes rich,
should I not be rejoicing over my thread-bare garments? Should I
not be giving out of my love? Indeed I ask, is it even possible to love
without giving?*

Day 327

Then our mouth was filled with laughter, and our
tongue with shouts of joy; then they said among the
nations, "The LORD has done great things for them."
—PSALM 126:2, ESV

*Lord, how joyful I am for You today. How You fill my soul with joy, my
mouth with laughter and place a smile on my face for You and me and
the world entire! I hope we make You happy too; I really, really do.*

Day 328

And my God will supply every need
of yours according to his riches
in glory in Christ Jesus.
—PHILIPPIANS 4:19, ESV

I never knew what my most pressing needs were until You met them. Having felt relief, I pray that Your Spirit guides me in meeting the needs of others, in healing like wounds, in sharing another's pain. O, Lord, how grateful I am for Your mercy and kindness!

Day 329

Our purpose is to please God ...
—1 THESSALONIANS 2:4

How do I affirm my created humanness, O God of my life? Is it not through my artistic self, my womanhood, my hunger for love, my thirst for You, and my intense desire to bow down and worship You that defines me as human? Is it possible I should want not to please You?

Day 330

... God has made this Jesus, whom you
crucified, to be both Lord and Messiah!
—ACTS 2:36

*How is it possible, Lord, for someone beaten and bruised, despised
and denied, ridiculed and made ragged two thousand years ago,
to gain a devoted following—a following that would grow into the
worldwide Church of today? Who stands out as Your people today? I
shudder to ask, do I?*

≈

Day 331

So now faith, hope, and love abide, these
three; but the greatest of these is love.
—1 CORINTHIANS 13:13, ESV

*You have taught me to love, God, You have! You have placed people
and children in my life who constantly inspire me to love better, to
respond with warmth, abandon, and surrender. By loving me, my Father, You have freed me to love! And I thank Thee from the bottom of
my heart.*

Day 332

So if there is any encouragement in Christ, any
comfort from love, any participation in the
Spirit, any affection and sympathy ...
—PHILIPPIANS 2:1, ESV

*You have taken hold complete hold of my emotions—from anguish
to cheer. The more my moods fluctuate the more constant You are!
Always You incline yourself to my heart. Where I am, You are, and for
this—for Your unchanging love, I praise and thank Thee.*

Day 333

All things were created in him. He created everything
in heaven and on earth. He created everything that
can be seen and everything that can't be seen. He
created kings, powers, rulers and authorities. All
things have been created by him and for him. 17
Before anything was created, he was already
there. He holds everything together.
—COLOSSIANS 1:17, NIRV

*You hold things all together. You hold me. Thus, to You be the glory
and honour forever. Amen.*

Day 334

Do not be conformed to this world, but be
transformed by the renewal of your mind, that
by testing you may discern what is the will of God,
what is good and acceptable and perfect.
—ROMANS 12:2, ESV

*Test me, O merciful God, and see if this countenance does not testify
to an inner tranquility of the mind, and of a soul willing to be turned
inside out by You. Strip away the old and renew me, Lord, that I may
boast of Your glory to times indefinite!*

Day 335

… my speech and my message were not in plausible
words of wisdom, but in demonstration of the Spirit
and of power, so that your faith might not rest in the
wisdom of men but in the power of God.
—1 CORINTHIANS 2:4–5

*Neither wit, nor words, nor action of my own can redeem or compel
a single soul to worship You. It is Your Spirit that fuels desire; Your
power that strengthens my will, and Your wisdom that I now commend for all to hear!*

Day 336

In the beginning was the Word, and the Word was
with God, and the Word was God.
—JOHN 1:1, NIV

*Shortest genealogy in the entire Word: "The Word was God," meaning
Jesus Christ, of course. Thank you for showing us yourself in Christ,
for being the bread of life, the light of the world, the good shepherd, the
resurrection and the life, the way the truth, and the life, the vine. My
God, how honoured I am to call You MINE!*

Day 337

I have learned the secret of being content
in any and every situation.
—PHILIPPIANS 4:12, NIV

*How tender is the letter of Philippians though Paul be imprisoned!
What immense cause he has to rejoice and delight whilst slogged
with persecution, for are You not "the secret" to his "being content in
every situation?" Lord, let me rediscover You that I shall not envy his
contentment!*

Day 338

For I am already being poured out as
a drink offering, and the time of
my departure has come.
—2 Timothy 4:6, ESV

Paul blesses Timothy and prays that Christ's message be declared in his own appointed way. Death is imminent, but for Paul it seems but an incident. The inspired light is fading from his face; his spirit is being poured out; he is about to receive his crown of glory. Lord, I pray too for strength likewise in fulfilling my role in the work Christ begun. Thank You, Father.

Day 339

In the last days, there will be ...

... clouds without water, carried about by the
winds; late autumn trees without fruit, twice
dead, pulled up by the roots; raging waves
of the sea, foaming up their own shame;
wandering stars for whom is reserved the
blackness of darkness forever ... mockers in
the last time who would walk according to
their own ungodly lusts. These ae sensual
persons, who cause divisions ... But you
...building yourselves up on your most
holy faith; praying in the Holy Spirit, keep
yourselves in the love of God; looking
for the mercy of our Lord Jesus
Christ unto eternal life.
—Jude 12–13, 18–21, NKJV

*O Light of my Love, be the sole object of my affections! Keep me from
harm. Keep me in You!*

Day 340

THE MAGFICAT: MARY'S SONG OF PRAISE
"Oh, how my soul praises the Lord. How my spirit
rejoices in God my Savior! For he took notice of
his lowly servant girl, and from now on all
generations will call me blessed."
—LUKE 1:46–48

*What kind of woman meets Your favour, Lord? Out of the countless
thousand women in Israel, You choose Mary to birth and to raise Your
Son. In her own self-descriptive words, she is a "lowly servant girl," not
wealthy, not from a prominent family, not particularly outstanding.
But, she is intensely spiritual—and thus, ideal. Thank you for this
illustrious example of faith!*

Day 341

But he wanted to justify himself, so he
asked Jesus, "And who is my neighbor?"
—LUKE 10:29, NIV

*I am sure You would tell me, Lord, that love for one's neighbour begins
in my home and extends outward. Truly, my closest neighbours are
those I live with—my children and spouse. So if I practice loving embrace here, establish hospitality from my own home, will I not, then,
feel more at ease widening out?*

Day 342

When you give a luncheon or dinner, do not invite
your friends, your brothers or sisters, your relatives,
or your rich neighbors; if you do, they may invite
you back and so you will be repaid.
—LUKE 14:12, NIV

*I can assist distant strangers, but have I first loved those in my nearest
terrain? Have I seen, felt, heard, responded to the needs of those in my
own backyard—in my own community, surrounding locale, province,
and nation? Let me begin here and expand my love, Lord. I know I
can do it.*

Day 343

He replied, "The man they call Jesus made some mud
and put it on my eyes. He told me to go to Siloam and
wash. So I went and washed, and then I could see."
—JOHN 9:11, NIV

*What is my role in helping the poor? How am I personally challenged
by this? Do I see God's work taking place both inside and outside the
four walls of churches and temples? Am I willing to get my hands
dirty as Christ did and enter the trenches in acts of charity, justice,
and compassion?*

Day 344

If you see your fellow Israelite's donkey or ox
fallen on the road, do not ignore it. Help
the owner get it to its feet.
—DEUTERONOMY 22:4, NIV

It is virtually impossible to not see signs of hopeless despair. Within our very nation, I see signs of collective despair. When will we see that pointing out the problem is no longer enough, and move toward acknowledging systematic failure in addressing issues of poverty and dejection, and then committing to make a difference? Yes, Father, when will I?

Day 345

... they walked with me ... and they
turned many from lives of sin.
—MALACHI 2:6

Were we to remove sexuality from the picture, we'd see that humans truly just crave companionship in another. We simply want someone to take us by the hand, help us cross those precarious bridges, and walk with us a while, thereafter. At the end of the day, what else matters?

Day 346

... and there before me was a great multitude that
no one could count, from every nation, tribe,
people and language, standing before
the throne and before the Lamb.
—REVELATION 7:9, NIV

*O, how I yearn for universality of faith—one that embraces all
groups, nations, languages, and cultures! I live for the day when hon-
est-hearted ones shall not look in from the cold but feel welcomed and
made to belong. We are a global neighbourhood of faith seekers. Can
we not unite?*

Day 347

You are the Messiah, the Son of the living God.
—MATTHEW 16:16

*I wonder how Jesus' grandparents were with this unplanned preg-
nancy. Were they admonishing, shameful, rejoicing? Did they fear
judgement by the community? Did they recognize Christ as Messiah,
Son of the living God, destined for greatness despite lowly beginnings?
Such lack of family support saddens me. However did Mary manage?*

Day 348

The second is this: "Love your neighbor as yourself."
There is no commandment greater than these.
—MARK 12:31, NIV

O, the willingness Jesus showed to recognize the humanity of any neighbour regardless of tribal boundaries! His moral concern began with His own and was then extended to surrounding cultures. From His example, how can I not view humanitarian aid as both the right and moral thing to do?

≈

Day 349

So when all these things begin to happen, stand
and look up, for your salvation is near!
—LUKE 21:28

Let us remember, but let us not live in the past. Christ's birth, life, death, and resurrection are reminders of Your good grace and boundless love. May we, now, have the grace to let go of past woe, and by Your Spirit embrace today, stand tall, and raise our eyes upward, for truly, our best days are yet to come.

Day 350

Confused and disturbed, Mary tried to think what the
angel could mean. "Don't be afraid, Mary," the angel
told her, "for you have found favor with God!"
—LUKE 1:29–30

*Whatever could You mean, asks Mary? How would she hide this
"pregnancy bump?" How is something this conspicuous, this embar-
rassing, this grand, NOT vexing?! No doubt she is burdened with
shame and torn between sadness and joy. Yet she has found favour in
Your eyes. O Lord, what reason for a woman to rejoice!*

Day 351

Your word is a lamp to guide my feet
and a light for my path.
—PSALM 119:105

*Poor soul, poor soul, where is that which will do you good? Is peace
not found in the blessing of Your Word? Does Your letter to the world
not shine like the sun, lift away our sorrows and bring us joy? Do Your
timeless sayings not bless me with light from, without, within? May
Your Word be upon my life and shine through my eyes like a candle
in the night.*

Day 352

He calmed the storm to a whisper
and stilled the waves.
—PSALM 107:29

This morning I suffered; at present I am calm, and this I owe to faith, simply to an act of faith. I can think of death and eternity without trouble. Over a deep sea of sorrow floats divine calm, a suavity which is the work of You alone. Nothing human comforts the soul, nothing upholds it. Your spirit alone soothes the mind, sets the spirit free, and fills my heart with peace, gratefully.

Day 353

Every year Jesus' parents went to Jerusalem for the
Passover festival. When [Jesus] came to the village
of Nazareth, his boyhood home, he went as usual
to the synagogue on the Sabbath and stood
up to read the Scriptures.
—LUKE 2:41; 4:16

O Father, so faithful, so diligent were Joseph and Mary in inculcating Yyour Word. There can be no doubt in our minds that You chose the right earthly parents for Your Son—such an example to draw from. I can only hope to carry this into my own child-raising efforts. Help me, please.

Day 354

I have set you an example that you should
do as I have done for you.
—JOHN 13:15, NIV

O, how I lament over human suffering and world poverty today. As a Christian, my Father, I desire a revolution of values based on compassion. I long to not let good intentions or the pouring out of financial resources suffice. As a part of Christ's body, I pray for Christians to lead the movement on poverty. Show us the way, Father, and let us promise to obey!

Day 355

Joseph, her fiancé, was a good man and did not want
to disgrace her publicly, so he decided to break the
engagement quietly. As he considered this, an angel
of the Lord appeared to him in a dream. "Joseph,
son of David," the angel said, "do not be afraid
to take Mary as your wife. For the child within
her was conceived by the Holy Spirit."
—MATTHEW 1:19–20

*Joseph, Jesus' adoptive father, engaged to a woman midst a potential
paternity scandal, has more reason to fearfully flee than any man
alive, but does not, for he has puts faith in "a dream." How exemplary
is he? Lord, grant me such trust, I pray!*

Day 356

This is why I weep and my eyes overflow with tears.
No one is near to comfort me, no one
to restore my spirit.
—LAMENTATIONS 1:16, NIV

*To know the comfort of another human being, to have You and the
companionship of Your Word, and to see individual beauty and worth
reflected from Your eyes is my blessing for each and every one of us
today, and every day. Amen.*

Day 357

For a child is born to us, a son is given to us. The
government will rest on his shoulders. And he
will be called: Wonderful Counselor, Mighty
God, Everlasting Father, Prince of Peace. The
passionate commitment of the Lord of
Heaven's Armies will make this happen!
—ISAIAH 9:6–7

A child is born under less than ideal circumstances—happens every day, right? Ah, but this birth is different. This is the birthing of promise. This child will redeem humanity, redeem lost potential, lost chance, lost hope: it is cause for reflection and praise, for by Your passion—yes, by Your passionate commitment to the human race, our past is forgiven, our present makes sense, and our future looks glorious. Today, let us not just herald the birth of a child, but laud our reigning King!

Day 358

... set your hope fully on the grace that will be
brought to you at the revelation of Jesus Christ.
—1 PETER 1:13, ESV

*O Merciful God, where would we be had Mary and Joseph not brave
or faithful been? Would my children have had the freedom to grow and
blossom into the people You designed them to be had this young couple
not believed in a dream? O that we all have such courage to believe!*

≈

Day 359

I will bless those who have humble and contrite
hearts, who tremble at my word.
—ISAIAH 66:2

The shepherds ... went back, glorifying and praising
God for all the things they had heard and seen.
—LUKE 2:20

*It isn't from the mouths of prominent Jewish members that Joseph
and Mary hear Jesus' birth confirmed by You, but from the mouth
of lowly shepherds. They hasten to do so, and are neither shocked nor
embarrassed the newborn Messiah is in a stable. Blessed, indeed, are
the humble!*

Day 360

...they offered the sacrifice required in
the law of the Lord—"either a pair of
turtledoves or two young pigeons."
—Luke 2:24

*This baby would not receive the finest life had to offer, but would sur-
pass all the hopes and dreams a mother and father could ever have for
a child. Truly, material assets matter not in parenting. It is our spiritual assets that do. O may this spirit of mine find favour with You!*

Day 361

What good is it, dear brothers and sisters, if you say
you have faith but don't show it by your actions?
Can that kind of faith save anyone?
—James 2:14

*Father, in Mary and Joseph, I see tremendous dignity in parenthood,
and thank You for this. I thank You for their faithful example of courage, dedication, and humble determination. Their lives are long gone,
but O, how their spirit lives on! Lord, I pray such a spirit define me.*

Day 362

Jesus looked at him and loved him. "One thing you
lack," he said. "Go, sell everything you have and
give to the poor, and you will have treasure
in heaven. Then come, follow me."
—MARK 10:21, NIV

*As individuals, as the Church of God, how can we reflect on global
economic despair and, in the spirit of heartfelt prayer, be stirred to
action? How will an enhanced love of justice incite us to challenge and
press political leaders toward creating change? Truly I ask, Lord, how
can Your sense of justice and compassion become mine?*

Day 363

… serve one another humbly in love.
—GALATIANS 5:13, NIV

*How can I get to know my neighbour? How authentically can I love
them? Lord, let me not just count the ways in which I can serve, but
serve! Open the eyes of my heart that I may not look away from suffering but embrace it, Lord. This I pray.*

Day 364

Their burnt offerings and sacrifices will be accepted
on my altar; for my house will be called a
house of prayer for all nations.
—ISAIAH 56:7, NIV

*No one should feel abandoned; no soul left behind. I cry out for col-
lective acceptance and collective embrace of impoverished people the
world over. I beg that political action accompanies open, honest dis-
cussion, and welcomes corporate prayer into the boardroom. Let us
seek Your voice and make it known, dear Lord.*

Day 365

Oh, that you had listened to my commands! Then you
would have had peace flowing like a gentle river and
righteousness rolling over you like waves in the sea.
—ISAIAH 48:18

*Read. Write. Pray. Take the hand of another and walk with them
on this homeward road. Fill my mind with peace like a river. Let me
dwell upon Your Word that the windows of my soul shall glow with
light calling me home, calling strangers, calling friends to shelter from
the storm.*

Also By Shauna May

Escaping the Smoke and Rain:
Moving Through and Beyond the Jehovah's Witness Community
978-1-4866-0277-3

Breaking free from the Jehovah's Witness community would be the
test that would become my testimony. There I was climbing the ice-
clad rungs of a rickety old ladder, anchored in a bed of snow, hang-
ing Christmas lights for the very first time. I was convinced no other
symbol would illumine my debut as brightly or as swiftly as this. It
felt exhilarating yet terrifying all at once—like standing on the edge
of a precipice fearing that stepping off would either plunge me into
death, or somehow, someway, teach me to fly.

Shauna May provides a revelatory look into the life of a religiously divided
family—her mother a fiercely zealous Jehovah's Witness, and her father
a geophysicist and self-professed atheist. Her father's death propels May
into a luminous quest for truth and freedom, a quest with a price attached:
to break out of the Order, she must break the ties that bind.

May enlightens the process of learning, unlearning, and relearning
certain basic truths while engaging in the struggle involved in walking
from and into life anew. Positively written, *Escaping the Smoke and Rain*
is an unforgettable testimony of the transformative power of spirituality.